2.95

The
Yogurt
Gourmet

The Yogurt Gourmet

by Anne Lanigan

Illustrations by Clifford Dennis

New York   London   Tokyo

International Standard Book Number: 0-8256-3129-7
Library of Congress Catalog Card Number: 78-69944

In Great Britain: Book Sales Ltd., 78 Newman Street, London W1.
In Canada: Gage Trade Publishing, P.O. Box 5000, 164 Com-
mander Blvd., Agincourt, Ontario M1S 3C7.

In Japan: Music Sales Corporation, 4-26-22 Jingumae, Shibuya-ku,
Tokyo 150.

Book design by Leslie Bauman.
Cover photo by Herbert Wise.

Contents

Introduction

When I started working on this cookbook, people to whom I mentioned it were curious about my involvement with yogurt in view of my background.

I grew up in New York City in a home where the food was basic American cooking. The only cookbook in the house was the *Boston Cooking School Cookbook.* My father had grown up in England, so a few traces of his background manifested themselves in the form of kippered herrings for breakfast. I should add that they were for his breakfast alone and I always knew when he was having them, as I would be awakened by their permeating smell, a smell I detested as much as I did the kippers. The only other Anglicism I remember was curried lamb, which I liked very much—undoubtedly the result of my paternal grandfather's service in India with the British Army.

Yogurt was not very well known when I was growing up, which seems hard to believe now, and I never tasted it until I was an adult. Like many people, I started with the fruit yogurts because I didn't like the tast of unflavored yogurt. However, I gradually developed an appreciation of plain yogurt and now rarely eat any of the flavored ones.

Some years ago I was given a yogurt maker and started experimenting with different formulas, using whole milk, skimmed milk, evaporated and powdered milks. An article on the Near Eastern practice of draining yogurt, forming it into small balls and storing it in oil started me on draining yogurt. First I drained it completely to make "yogurt cheese" and then I began draining it partially to use as a substitute for sour cream. Then a series of experiments developed in cooking with yogurt and utilizing it in all sorts of foods, including the obvious one of cold soups. I found that in some dishes the tartness of the yogurt enhanced the basic flavor of the food and added a subtlety of flavor—as in the sauce base for Cheese Soufflé. In other foods, such as baked goods, the taste was unnoticeable.

In this collection of recipes I have attempted very little in the realm of ethnic foods. Lacking a grandmother who was Armenian or Greek or Indian I have left those areas to others more qualified than I.

I have enjoyed working on this book and hope that you too will enjoy making yogurt an increasingly used ingredient in your cooking. I am sure there are untold ways of using it that I have not covered, but I shall go on experimenting, and hope you do too.

This book is dedicated to my friends as an expression of my deep appreciation for all their help while I was working on it—for their suggestions, ideas, criticisms, information and encouragement, to say nothing of their patience in tasting and judging and sampling. Like practically everything else in life, it could not have worked without them.

The Yogurt Gourmet

Yogurt and How to Make It

Simply defined, yogurt is milk that has been curdled to the consistency of custard by the addition of lactic-acid-producing cultures, such as lactobacillus bulgaricus, lactobacillus yoghurt and streptococcus thermophilus. When one or more of these cultures is added to warm milk, which is then allowed to remain warm and undisturbed for a period of five hours or more, the result is yogurt.

Many forms of this fermented milk have been known throughout history, going back to the early nomadic tribesmen of Asia and southeastern Europe. It is also known in Scandinavia, Africa and South America. Early references to it were made by the second-century Greek physician Galen, and are also found in early Arabic writings on medicine.

Yogurt is made from the milk of a cow, sheep, goat, buffalo, or even a mare. The last is used by the nomadic tribes of Lapland, southern Russia and parts of Asia. Called by various names *(paiura, kefir* and *koumiss)*, it is highly acidic, alcoholic and effervescent.

Therapeutic Qualities of Yogurt

Yogurt was widely publicized as beneficial by the work of Elie Metchnikoff, co-winner of the 1908 Nobel Prize. In his research at the Pasteur Institute in Paris, he was impressed by the longevity of some of the Bulgarians and attributed it to the large amounts of yogurt in their diet. He studied the effects of lactic-acid bacteria on the digestive tract in preventing putrification.

Although its effect on longevity has not been proven, yogurt does have proven beneficial properties. It is more easily and more quickly digested than plain milk. It helps maintain the necessary bacteria, or flora, in the intestinal tract. That is the reason many doctors prescribe yogurt for patients who are taking antibiotics, which can destroy the natural flora in the system. It is also thought that yogurt can help prevent bacterial infection.

A recent report by medical researchers who worked with the Masai tribe in Africa raises the provocative theory that there may be something in yogurt that inhibits the buildup of cholesterol. To test the effect on cholesterol levels of surfactants (food additives that prevent separation in mixtures) they worked with two groups. One group had the surfactant added to its yogurt-like fermented milk; the other group did not. Both groups consumed larger quantities than usual of this yogurt (a part of their normal diet) and both groups gained weight, which usually raises the cholesterol level. Much to the surprise of the researchers, although the cholesterol level of the surfactant group was higher than that of the other group, both groups had lower cholesterol levels than before the test. Further research will have to be done to confirm this finding.

So there you have yogurt. Reputedly beneficial, historic, and still going strong. Apart from all that, however, is the incontrovertible fact that it tastes good!

Best of all, though, is homemade yogurt. Apart from the fact that it saves a lot of money to make your own, it is easy to make and great to cook with.

Making Yogurt

Yogurt is made by adding yogurt culture to warm milk and allowing the mixture to remain warm and undisturbed for a minimum of 5 hours. The 5-hour incubation period produces a very mild yogurt; the tartness increases with longer incubation.

Yogurt can be made with or without a machine; in either case the basic process is the same. Milk is scalded (heated to just below the boiling point) and cooled to a temperature of 110° before the culture is added to the milk. The yogurt culture can be killed if exposed to a temperature of 125° and can become dormant below 90°.

The yogurt culture consists of either plain (unflavored) yogurt or a dry yogurt starter. The dry starter is sold in health food stores and makes 1 quart. The plain yogurt can be regular or low fat yogurt.

The milk can be whole or skimmed. If using skimmed milk, you will need to add powdered non-fat milk to achieve a satisfactory result. (If you check the labels on low-fat yogurts you will note this is done commercially.) Yogurt can also be made from powdered or canned milk. The creamiest yogurt is made from whole milk. (The creamiest of all is made from whole milk to which a little cream has been added!)

The quantity you make is limited only by the size of your bowls (or pots) and oven.

I use both the yogurt machine and the bulk process. I like the convenience of individual jars of yogurt for eating (particularly if there's more than one person eating it). I like a larger quantity for cooking, and for draining to make thickened yogurt and yogurt cheese.

Here's how to make yogurt.

INGREDIENTS
1 quart whole milk, or 1 quart skim milk plus ½ cup powdered non-fat milk (added after milk has been heated)
2 tablespoons plain yogurt (regular or low-fat)

Note: Powdered or canned milk can also be used.

EQUIPMENT
Thermometer (candy or deep fry)
Large mixing bowl or pitcher
Measuring spoon or coffee measure
Small bowl or cup
Large spoon or wire whisk

If you are not using a yogurt machine, you will need a large clean jar (or several jars) or a bowl of glass, metal or plastic, in which the mixture will incubate. In a saucepan, heat the milk over a moderate flame to just below the boiling point (195°). If it should boil, by accident, it will not affect the flavor or the finished product.

When the milk has reached 195°, pour it into a large bowl or pitcher and let it cool to 110°. If you can hold your finger in the milk for a count of 10 without saying "ouch," it has probably cooled enough.

Measure the 2 tablespoons of yogurt into a small bowl or cup. Add 2 or 3 tablespoons of warm milk and stir gently to dilute the yogurt. Add a little more milk and stir to mix thoroughly; add this to the rest of the milk. Stir gently with a large spoon or wire whisk to blend the yogurt thoroughly with the milk. Do this quickly so the milk does not cool down—the temperature of the milk is an essential part of the yogurt-making process. If the milk is too warm when the yogurt is added (say 125°) the culture cannot live. It is also important that you measure the yogurt with reasonable accuracy. Too much yogurt interferes with the growth of the culture and you will end up with sour, watery yogurt.

When the milk and yogurt have been thoroughly mixed, let the mixture remain warm and undisturbed for at least 5 hours. Longer incubation makes yogurt more tangy.

YOGURT MACHINE
If you are using a machine, pour or ladle the cultured milk into the individual jars and set the timer (if you have an automatic machine) for 5 hours. At the end of that time refrigerate the yogurt for 3 hours before using.

MACHINELESS YOGURT
There are many simple methods of keeping the yogurt warm for the incubation period. Two of the most effective tools I have found are a sheet of bubble plastic (often used in packing fragile items) and a bath towel. Various ways of using them are described below.

Oven. If you have a pilot in your oven which is permanently on, the heat generated by it is sufficient to maintain the even, gentle temperature that yogurt requires. Pour the warm-milk-and-yogurt mixture into a large clean jar (a large peanut butter jar holds a quart), bowl or covered casserole. Cover the jar or bowl with a piece of foil, wrap a bath towel around it, and place it in the oven. Let it remain undisturbed overnight or at least 5 hours. Refrigerate for 3 hours before using.

Water Bath. Fill a large pan that has a cover with enough hot water (150° to 160°) to come almost to the top of the jar or bowl in which you will be incubating the yogurt mixture. (Measure this before filling the bowl or jar with milk.) Pour the warm-milk-and-yogurt mixture in a large jar or bowl and place it in the hot water. Cover the top of the jar or bowl with foil or a paper towel.

Put the cover on the pan. Wrap a sheet of bubble plastic around the pan, and then wrap it with a bath towel. Leave undisturbed overnight or at least 5 hours. Refrigerate for 3 hours before using.

Heating Pad or Hot Water Bottle. Line a small carton or container (a wastebasket will work) with a bath towel. Pour the warm-milk-and-yogurt mixture into a large jar or bowl. Wrap a piece of bubble plastic around the jar or bowl and place it in the carton. Cover the jar or bowl with the ends of the towel and place a heating pad (set on low) on top. Or wrap a hot water bottle in a towel and place it next to the jar. Cover the top of the carton with another towel or some newspaper. Leave undisturbed overnight or at least 5 hours. Refrigerate for 3 hours before using.

Insulated Food Carrier or Ice Bucket. Warm the interior of an insulated carrier by rinsing it in very hot water. Line it with a bath towel. Pour the warm-milk-and-yogurt mixture into a large jar or bowl. Wrap a piece of bubble plastic around the jar or bowl and place it in the container. Wrap a bath towel around the plastic. Close the container and leave the mixture undisturbed overnight or at least 5 hours. Refrigerate for 3 hours before using.

Draining Yogurt

If yogurt is drained through several layers of cheesecloth (or a muslin bag), it becomes thicker as the whey drains off. When all the whey has drained, the resulting curd is a solid mass with the consistency of cream cheese. This process takes about 8 or 9 hours (convenient to do overnight). However, the greatest proportion of whey drains off in the first hour. If you let yogurt drain for only 5 or 10 minutes, you will remove a surprising amount of whey. A cup of yogurt gives up 25 percent of its volume in 5 minutes; a pint gives up 18 percent and a quart only 12 percent.

Place a strainer or colander over a bowl and line the strainer with 2 or 3 layers of cheesecloth that has been rinsed in cold water and wrung out. Put the yogurt in the lined strainer and let it drain. Or line a bowl with cheesecloth and put the yogurt in it.

Then form a pouch by pulling up the corners of the cloth and tying them together. Suspend this pouch from the kitchen faucet, and let the yogurt drain into the sink. Or fasten a cup hook on the underside of a kitchen cabinet and suspend the pouch from it, placing a bowl underneath to catch the whey. Or fasten the pouch to the handle of a kitchen cabinet door, suspend it from a pot hook, etc.

The clear, pale golden whey can be drunk alone or in combination with vegetable juices (there is a bottled carrot juice and whey on the market). It can also be used for cooking rice.

Cooking with Yogurt

Yogurt is like sour cream in that it will separate if allowed to boil. Separation in no way affects the flavor, but it can be prevented by using flour, cornstarch or arrowroot in sauces. Yogurt can be substituted for sour cream in any recipe (with far fewer calories, too). It can also be substituted for milk in many recipes, particularly in baking. When substituting yogurt for milk, however, add baking soda to the flour (½ teaspoon for each cup of yogurt).

Definitions of Terms

Drained Yogurt. Yogurt that has drained for about 10 minutes.
Thick Yogurt. Yogurt that has drained for at least 30 minutes. It will be thick but still soft—it will not retain its shape on a flat surface or the mark of a finger indentation. One hour's draining is ideal.
Yogurt Cheese. Yogurt that has drained for 8 hours or longer. It is the consistency of cream cheese, will hold its shape and retain the mark of a finger indentation.
Yogurt Cream. Heavy cream made into yogurt by the addition of 1 teaspoon of yogurt to ½ pint of cream. Exactly like crème fraiche!

Note: One quart of yogurt will yield approximately 1 1/3 cups of yogurt cheese (about 2 cups of whey is drained off). One quart of yogurt will yield about 2½ cups of thick yogurt (about 1¼ cups of whey is drained off).

Troubleshooting

Because yogurt contains living organisms, you will find, when making your own, that different batches often vary. There may even be times when the culture does not seem to work and you end up with milk rather than yogurt. To insure best results, check the following factors:

• If the milk is not fresh, it will have an adverse effect on the finished product. If the milk is too warm when the yogurt is added, the culture can be killed. The ideal temperature is 110°. At 125° the culture can be killed.

• If the milk cools off too much during incubation, the culture is inhibited and you end up with milk, rather than yogurt. If so, you can warm the milk (in its container) slightly and incubate it again in a warmer spot or with better insulation.

• If the starter is too old, you will end up with milk. There isn't anything to be done in this case except start over with fresh milk and fresh starter.

• If you have added too much yogurt to the milk, the result will be a sour, watery yogurt because the culture is "crowded."

• If the containers in which the yogurt will incubate are not clean, the bacteria in them can interfere with the yogurt culture and you will end up with milk.

So you need:
1. Fresh milk
2. Proper temperature—110°
3. Fresh starter
4. Proper amount of starter—2 tablespoons per quart of milk
5. Clean incubating jars or bowls
6. Proper incubation time—a minimum of 5 hours—with the mixture kept warm and undisturbed.

Hors d'Oeuvres and Appetizers

Quick and Easy Appetizers

ARTICHOKES
Serve cold cooked frozen artichoke hearts or rinsed and drained canned ones. Cut them in halves and toss them with diced ham or diced cooked chicken or turkey. Top with Mustard Dressing or Dill Dressing (see pages 156 and 157).

ASPARAGUS
Serve cold cooked asparagus spears with Vinaigrette Dressing (see page 157). Garnish each serving with a little sieved hard-cooked egg.

EGGPLANT
Scoop out the pulp from a large baked or steamed eggplant and mash it up well with a teaspoon of lemon juice, a cup of yogurt and salt and pepper. Sauté about 2 cups sliced onions very slowly over low heat until they are soft and brown. Spoon the onions over the eggplant and serve with French, Italian or pita bread.

FISH
Cut up cold leftover fish into small pieces. Serve on lettuce leaves with Dill Dressing (see page 156) or with a combination of yogurt and mayonnaise (½ cup each) and a teaspoon of capers. Or flake the contents of a can of tuna fish or salmon, toss with sliced cucumbers and serve with either of the above dressings.

Avocado Dip

1 medium avocado, pitted and peeled
1 teaspoon lemon juice
1 tablespoon grated onion (or to taste)
Salt to taste
½ cup drained yogurt**
Few drops tabasco (optional)

Mash the avocado with the lemon juice and onion. Add salt, drained yogurt and tabasco. Serve with corn chips or rice crackers.

Yield: 1 cup.

**See page 16.

Blue Cheese Dip

1 cup drained yogurt**
4 ounces blue cheese, crumbled
1 to 2 teaspoons Worcestershire
Salt to taste

Blend all ingredients and chill for several hours before serving. Serve with crackers.

Note: This can be varied by using undrained yogurt to make a more liquid dip for raw vegetables.

Yield: 1½ cups.

**See page 16.

Green Vegetable Dip

The exact ingredients for this cannot be given but they can be anything fresh and green that you have in your refrigerator. Use such items as the main stem from broccoli, fresh spinach, broccoli or cauliflower leaves, watercress, parsley, celery leaves, fresh herbs, lettuce, the core of a cabbage head, etc. Puree all together and season with salt, pepper, lemon juice, chopped scallions, dash of tabasco, etc. When all ingredients are pureed, blend in enough yogurt cheese** or thick yogurt** to give the consistency you want, depending on whether it is to be served as a dip for vegetables or corn chips, or as a spread for crackers or bread.

**See page 16.

Chicken Liver Pâté

4 tablespoons butter
1 pound chicken livers
½ pound mushrooms, sliced
½ cup scallions, thinly sliced, with part of tops
1 teaspoon salt
½ cup dry white wine or dry vermouth
1 clove garlic, minced or crushed
½ teaspoon dry mustard
¼ teaspoon dried rosemary
¼ teaspoon dried dill weed
¼ cup yogurt cheese**

In a large heavy pan, melt the butter and add the chicken livers, mushrooms, scallions and salt. Sauté for 5 minutes, stirring occasionally. Livers should still be slightly pink and tender.

Add the wine, garlic, mustard, rosemary and dill. Cover and simmer over low heat for about 10 minutes. Uncover the pan and raise heat to cook down the liquid until it is almost cooked away.

Let cool briefly. Place in blender and puree. Add the yogurt cheese and blend it in thoroughly.

Pack in 1 large crock or several smaller ones and chill for at least 8 hours before serving. Keeps about 2 weeks under refrigeration. After it is chilled, film the top with a thin layer of melted butter if you wish to prolong its storage life.

Serve with thin sliced bread, melba toast or crackers.

Yield: 2½ cups.

**See page 16.

Mock Liver Pâté

½ pound liverwurst
½ cup yogurt cheese**
¼ cup thick yogurt**
1½ tablespoons melted butter
1½ tablespoons Madeira, sherry or cognac
½ teaspoon curry powder (or to taste)
1 tablespoon Worcestershire sauce

Blend all ingredients thoroughly; chill for several hours. Serve with thin slices of dark bread, or crackers.

Note: This is better prepared in advance so flavors mellow.

Yield: 2 cups.

**See page 16.

Beef Horseradish Spread

One 2½ ounce jar dried chipped beef
1 cup yogurt cheese**
1 tablespoon prepared horseradish (or to taste)

Rinse beef and dry thoroughly. Shred it coarsely (using scissors is the easiest way). Add yogurt cheese and horseradish. Blend thoroughly. Serve with party rye or crackers.

Yield: 1½ cups.

**See page 16.

Smoked Salmon Spread

2 ounces smoked salmon
1 cup yogurt cheese**
½ teaspoon dried dill
Pepper to taste

Shred the salmon coarsely (using scissors is the easiest way). Blend with yogurt cheese and seasonings. Serve with crackers or melba toast.

Yield: 1½ cups.

**See page 16.

Cheese Wafers

¼ pound butter (1 stick)
4 ounces sharp cheese, grated
½ cup yogurt cheese**
1¾ cups all-purpose flour
½ teaspoon salt
¼ to ½ teaspoon cayenne pepper

Cream the butter and cheeses together. Work in the flour, salt and cayenne. Form into a roll. Wrap in wax paper and chill thoroughly.

Preheat the oven to 375°.

Slice dough thinly and bake on a cookie sheet in the upper third of the oven for about 10 minutes or until golden.

Yield: 5 dozen.

**See page 16.

Eggplant Puree

1 medium eggplant, about 1½ pounds
2 tablespoons olive oil
1 cup yogurt
1 tablespoon lemon juice (or to taste)
1 or 2 cloves garlic, minced
Salt to taste
2 tablespoons minced parsley

Pierce the eggplant in several places and bake in a preheated 350° oven for about an hour. Or steam the eggplant in a steamer or sieve set over boiling water in a tightly covered pot for about 15 to 20 minutes or until soft.

When the eggplant is cool enough to handle, peel it. Chop the pulp, mashing it well. Mix with the other ingredients, or puree everything in a food processor or blender. Taste and adjust seasonings—over-season somewhat, as it will be served cold.

Chill for several hours. Serve with thinly sliced dark bread, melba toast or crackers.

Yield: 2½ cups.

Apple and Crabmeat

One 6-ounce package frozen crabmeat, thawed, or
*   one 6½-ounce can or 1 cup fresh cooked crabmeat*
2 or 3 firm eating apples
1 tablespoon lemon juice mixed with
*   2 cups cold water*
½ cup thick yogurt**
½ cup mayonnaise
2 tablespoons minced parsley or watercress,
*   1 tablespoon fresh dill, or 1 teaspoon dried dill*
Salt and pepper to taste

Few drops lemon juice
Lettuce leaves
Tomatoes

Drain the crabmeat, if necessary. Peel and core the apples and either slice them or cut them into small cubes. As you cut the apples, drop the pieces into the acidulated water to prevent discoloration.

Mix the thick yogurt with the mayonnaise and whatever green herb you are using in a large bowl. Add the crabmeat and toss lightly. Drain the apples thoroughly and pat them dry. Toss them with the crabmeat mixture.

Taste and correct seasoning with a dash of salt and pepper or a few drops of lemon juice.

Serve on lettuce leaves. A cherry tomato or two or a slice of tomato would make a nice garnish.

Yield: 4 to 6 servings.

**See page 16.

Stuffed Artichoke Bottoms

Imported 14-ounce cans of artichoke bottoms (called *fonds d'artichauts* and available in fancy food departments) are a useful item to have on hand. They are packed in brine or acidulated water and should be washed off before using, whether they are served cold or hot.

COLD ARTICHOKE BOTTOMS WITH SHRIMP FILLING
1 pound cooked, peeled and deveined shrimp
½ cup diced celery or ½ cup diced water chestnuts
Salt and pepper to taste
Dash of lemon juice
Dill or Curry Dressing (see page 156)
One 14-ounce can artichoke bottoms
Lettuce leaves
Black olives or cherry tomatoes

Cut the shrimp into 2 to 4 pieces each, depending on size.

Toss the shrimp with the celery or water chestnuts and the salt, pepper, lemon juice and dressing.

Wash the artichoke bottoms and pat them dry. Allowing one per serving, place on lettuce leaves and top each one with the shrimp filling. Garnish with black olives or cherry tomatoes.

Yield: 6 to 8 servings.

COLD ARTICHOKE BOTTOMS WITH MUSHROOM FILLING
½ pound mushrooms
Salt and pepper to taste
1 or 2 ripe tomatoes, about ½ pound
2 teaspoons lemon juice (or to taste)
½ cup thick yogurt**
½ cup mayonnaise
One 14-ounce can artichoke bottoms
Lettuce leaves

Wipe the mushrooms with a damp paper towel. Slice off the stems (save them for use in stews, soups, Duxelles (page 161), etc.). Thinly slice the mushroom caps, and sprinkle lightly with a little salt and pepper.

Slice the tomatoes. Mix the lemon juice, thick yogurt and mayonnaise.

Wash the artichoke bottoms and pat them dry. Arrange them on lettuce leaves allowing one per serving. Pile raw mushroom slices on the artichokes and cover them with 1 or 2 tomato slices. Top each with a large dollop of the yogurt-and-mayonnaise mixture.

Yield: 6 to 8 servings.

**See page 16.

HOT ARTICHOKE BOTTOMS

One 14-ounce can contains 6 to 8 bottoms. Wash the artichoke bottoms. Place them in 1 layer in a large saucepan or skillet with about 1/8 inch water. Add a pat or two of butter. Cover the pan and let the artichoke bottoms cook very gently over very low heat until they are hot.

Serve them on toast rounds filled with
1. Mushrooms au Gratin (see page 116; divide the recipe in half)
2. Mushroom Sauce (see page 162)
3. Poached egg topped with Bearnaise Sauce (see page 165)
4. Cut-up shrimp topped with Mornay Sauce (see page 160)

Celery Root Appetizer

1 or 2 celery roots (about 1 pound)
1 tablespoon lemon juice
1 teaspoon salt, or boiling water
1 egg
2 teaspoons lemon juice
½ teaspoon salt (or to taste)
1/8 teaspoon pepper (or to taste)
Pinch of sugar
1 tablespoon Dijon-type mustard
*1 to 1½ cups thick yogurt***
2 to 3 tablespoons minced parsley or
*   mixed fresh green herbs*
Black olives or radishes

Peel the celery roots and cut them into julienne strips or shred them coarsely. (There should be about 3 to 3½ cups.) Tenderize the celery root by either tossing with the 1 tablespoon lemon juice and 1 teaspoon salt and letting them marinate for about 30 minutes, or blanch in boiling water for about 1 minute. If marinating in lemon juice, rinse the strips in cold water after 30 minutes and pat dry with a towel. If blanching them, pat them dry and let cool briefly.

In a mixing bowl, beat the egg well and add the 2 teaspoons lemon juice, ½ teaspoon salt, the pepper and sugar. Beat in the mustard and mix well. Add 1 cup of the thick yogurt and mix well. Taste and adjust seasonings.

Toss the celery root with the dressing to coat it lightly but thoroughly. If necessary, add a bit more thick yogurt, but be sparing. The strips should just be lightly coated with dressing.

Refrigerate for several hours or overnight. Serve sprinkled with the parsley or herbs. Black olives or radishes or both make an attractive garnish.

Yield: 6 servings.

**See page 16.

VARIATIONS
Add sliced raw mushrooms to the celery root before tossing with the dressing.
Substitute Mustard Dressing or Vinaigrette Dressing (page 157) for the yogurt dressing.

Leeks Vinaigrette

1 or 2 bunches of leeks (see Note)
½ teaspoon Dijon-type mustard
1 tablespoon white wine vinegar or lemon juice
Salt and pepper to taste
3 tablespoons olive oil
½ cup drained yogurt**
Lettuce leaves

Trim the bottoms of the leeks and cut off enough of the green tops to make the leeks a uniform length. With a sharp knife, make several cuts lengthwise in the green tops (2 cuts for small ones and 3 for large ones). Wash the leeks thoroughly under cold running water. Spread the leaves apart with your fingers to remove all traces of sand. Tie the ends of the leeks lightly to keep their shape, and place them in boiling salted water to cover. Cover the pan and simmer for about 25 to 35 minutes until the white part of the leek is soft and tender. Drain the leeks thoroughly and let them cool slightly.

Add the mustard to the vinegar or lemon juice and stir to dissolve it thoroughly. Add the salt, pepper and olive oil and mix well.

Add the drained yogurt and beat well.

Place the leeks in a flat dish and pour the dressing over them. Refrigerate for several hours. Serve on lettuce leaves.

Note: The size of leeks varies greatly. Allow 2 large or 3 small leeks per person.

Yield: 4 servings.

**See page 16.

Salmon Mousse

1 envelope unflavored gelatin
2 tablespoons dry white wine or dry vermouth
1 tablespoon lemon juice
¼ cup boiling water
2 tablespoons minced shallots, or 1 tablespoon
   minced onion
1 tablespoon butter
1 cup cooked salmon, or minced
   7¾-ounce can salmon
½ cup thick yogurt**
½ cup mayonnaise
Salt and pepper to taste
Few drops tabasco
Black olives

In a small bowl, soften the gelatin in wine or vermouth and lemon juice, and add the boiling water.

In a small pan, sauté the shallots or onion in the butter for about 2 minutes over low heat; do not let them brown. Add the gelatin mixture and simmer for a minute or so until the gelatin is completely dissolved.

If using canned salmon, drain it and remove the skin and bones (if you are fortunate enough to own a food processor, the bones can be left in).

In a blender or food processor, puree the salmon and add the gelatin-and-shallot mixture. Puree briefly. Add the ½ cup thick yogurt and ½ cup mayonnaise, and blend until the mixture is completely smooth. Add the seasonings, taste and adjust. Over-season slightly, as the chilling will mask the seasonings.

Lightly oil a 2-cup mold and turn the salmon mixture into it. Cover the mold with wax paper and refrigerate for several hours or overnight.

Unmold and serve with dill dressing (see page 156).

Garnish with black olives.

Yield: 4 to 6 servings.

**See page 16.

Souffléd Mushrooms

1½ pounds mushrooms
¼ cup vegetable oil
2 tablespoons butter
¼ cup minced onions
1 tablespoon flour
½ cup yogurt
2 eggs, separated
½ cup minced cooked ham or chicken
Salt and pepper to taste

Preheat the oven to 375°.

Wash the mushrooms and pat dry. Remove stems (save for use in sauces, soups and Duxelles—page 161) and brush the caps with the oil. Place caps top side down on a baking sheet and set aside.

In a saucepan, melt the butter and sauté the onions over medium low heat until they are soft (but not brown), about 3 or 4 minutes. Sprinkle the flour on the onion and cook, stirring for about 2 or 3 minutes. Add the yogurt and stir until the sauce comes to a boil. Let it cook gently for a minute or two and then remove it from the heat. Cool slightly.

Beat the egg yolks and add to them the minced ham or chicken. Add this mixture to the slightly cooled sauce, mix well and season to taste with salt and pepper.

Beat the egg whites until they form soft peaks. Fold half of them gently into the sauce mixture. Quickly fold in the rest of the whites and fill the mushroom caps with the mixture.

Bake in the lower third of the oven for about 12 minutes. Serve hot.

Yield: 4 to 6 servings.

Soups

Cold Avocado Soup

1 large or 2 medium ripe avocados
1 tablespoon lemon or lime juice
1½ cup chicken broth
1 cup plain yogurt
Salt and pepper to taste
Pinch of cayenne pepper or few drops
    tabasco (optional)
Minced fresh dill or chives

Peel and chop the avocados (there should be 1 cup) and mash with the lemon or lime juice. Puree in a blender with the chicken broth. Add the yogurt and seasonings and blend very briefly. Chill thoroughly.

Sprinkle with fresh dill or chives.

Yield: 4 servings.

VARIATION
Substitute curry powder to taste for the cayenne or tabasco.

Armenian Barley Soup

1 cup barley
6 cups beef or chicken stock
4 tablespoons butter
¾ cup chopped onion
¼ cup chopped parsley
1/3 cup chopped fresh mint, or
    1 tablespoon dried mint
Salt and pepper to taste
4 cups yogurt

Cook the barley in the stock over low heat for about an hour. In a saucepan, melt the butter over low heat and sauté the onion until soft and translucent but not brown. Add the onion to the barley. Add the parsley and mint, and cook over low heat for about 30 minutes. Add salt and pepper to taste.

When the barley is tender, mix about ½ cup of the stock from the pot with the yogurt, then stir the yogurt gradually into the soup and lower the heat. Simmer the soup for a minute or two, stirring gently to blend.

Serve the soup immediately or chill it and serve cold.

Yield: 6 to 8 servings.

VARIATION
Substitute 1 cup long-grain rice for the barley.

Note: This soup is an Armenian standby and appears in almost identical form in many books on Armenian cooking.

Chilled Green Bean Soup

1 pound string beans
2 tablespoons minced scallions
2 teaspoons salt
2 tablespoons flour
1½ cups yogurt
2 tablespoons white wine vinegar
1 tablespoon sugar
1/8 teaspoon nutmeg
Thick yogurt**
Chopped mint leaves

Trim the beans and cut them into pieces about ½ inch long. Put the beans and minced scallions in a saucepan with about 1½ quarts (6 cups) boiling salted water. Cook the beans, covered, for about 15 to 20 minutes, or until they are tender.

When the beans are cooked, reserve 1 quart (4 cups) of the cooking liquid and discard the rest. Return all but ½ cup of the reserved cooking liquid to the pot with the beans.

Combine the flour with ½ cup cooking liquid to make a paste. Add this to the yogurt, blending well. Combine this mixture with the beans and the cooking liquid, stirring to blend. Simmer the soup for about 5 minutes and add the vinegar, sugar and nutmeg. Taste and adjust seasonings, and remove soup from heat.

Chill well and garnish each serving with a dollop of thick yogurt and a sprinkling of chopped mint leaves.

Yield: 4 servings.

**See page 16.

Cream of Broccoli Soup

1 bunch broccoli (about 1½ pounds)
½ cup cooked macaroni or diced cooked potato
1 cup chicken stock
Salt and pepper to taste
Pinch of nutmeg
1 cup yogurt
Lemon slices (for cold soup)

Cut the stems off the broccoli and peel them. Cut them into large pieces and place in a heavy pan with boiling salted water. Cook for about 5 minutes. Add the florets (reserve a few for garnish) and cook for about 5 minutes longer, or until tender.

Drain the broccoli and puree it in a blender. Add the macaroni or potato and the chicken stock, and blend thoroughly. Add the salt, pepper and nutmeg. Taste and adjust seasonings.

If you are serving the soup hot, return it to the pan and heat it over low heat. Add the yogurt and heat it for a few minutes over very low heat. Do not let it boil. Garnish with reserved florets.

If serving it cold, add the yogurt to the blender and blend briefly. Chill the soup thoroughly and garnish each serving with a lemon slice topped with a bit of broccoli floret.

Yield: 6 servings.

Cold Cream of Carrot Soup

1 pound carrots (about 5 large)
3 tablespoons butter
¼ cup minced onion
1 stalk celery, chopped
1 medium potato, diced
Pinch of nutmeg
Salt to taste
4 cups chicken broth
Pinch of cayenne pepper
¼ teaspoon dried chervil
1 cup yogurt

Wash and scrape the carrots and chop them coarsely.

In a heavy pan, melt the butter and add the onion, carrots, celery and potato. Cook, stirring, for about 5 minutes. Add the nutmeg, salt and 2 cups of the chicken broth. Add the cayenne and chervil. Cook over low heat and simmer for about 30 minutes, until vegetables are soft.

Remove pan from heat; taste and adjust seasonings. Puree the soup in a blender with the remaining 2 cups of broth. Add the yogurt and blend briefly. Refrigerate for several hours.

Serve with any of the following garnishes: diced pimiento, shredded carrot which has been blanched briefly in boiling water or chopped hard-boiled egg and minced parsley.

Yield: 6 servings.

Cream of Cauliflower Soup

1 medium head cauliflower (about 1½ pounds)
    or 3 cups cooked cauliflower
1 tablespoon butter
2 tablespoons chopped onion
1½ cups chicken broth
½ teaspoon salt(or to taste)
¼ teaspoon pepper (preferably white)
½ teaspoon nutmeg
Dash of tabasco (optional)
2 cups yogurt
2 tablespoons minced watercress or parsley

If using fresh cauliflower, trim it and soak it in cold salted water for about 20 minutes. Cut off the stem and chop it into large pieces. Break up the florets.

In a heavy pan, melt the butter over low heat and add the chopped onion. Sauté the onion until it is soft and wilted but not brown. Add the chicken broth, bring it just to a boil and add the cauliflower stems. Cook over low heat for about 5 minutes, then add the florets and cook another 15 minutes, or until the cauliflower is tender. If using cooked cauliflower, add it with the chicken broth and then blend.

Let the cauliflower and broth cool slightly, then puree in a blender. Add the salt, pepper, nutmeg and tabasco, and puree briefly. Taste and adjust seasonings. Add the yogurt and puree briefly.

If you are serving the soup hot, return it to the pan to reheat. Do not let it boil.

If you are serving the soup cold, refrigerate it for several hours to chill thoroughly.

Garnish each serving with a little minced watercress or parsley.

Yield: 4 to 6 servings.

Chicken and Clam Consommé

4 cups chicken stock
One 15-ounce can of clam-and-tomato juice
2 cloves garlic
2 tablespoons dry white wine or
   dry vermouth (optional)
1 large strip of lemon peel
1 bay leaf
Salt, if necessary
1 teaspoon grated lemon rind
2 tablespoons minced parsley
*½ cup thick yogurt** or*
   *whipped yogurt cream***

In a heavy pan, combine the chicken stock and Clamato or clam juice with the garlic, wine or vermouth, lemon peel, bay leaf and salt. Bring almost to a boil, then let simmer for about 15 minutes. Remove the garlic and bay leaf, and discard them. Taste and adjust seasonings.

While the soup is simmering, combine lemon rind and parsley with the thick yogurt or whipped yogurt cream.

Ladle the soup into individual soup bowls and top each with a tablespoon of the yogurt mixture.

Yield: 6 servings.

**See page 16.

Cold Cucumber Soup

1 large or 2 small cucumbers, 1 pound
(2 cups peeled and diced)
Salt
2 or 3 cloves garlic
3 to 4 cups plain yogurt
3 tablespoons minced fresh mint, or
1 tablespoon crushed dried mint
Pepper

Put the cucumbers in a bowl and sprinkle with salt. Add a few ice cubes and let the cucumbers sit in the iced salted water for 30 minutes.

Mash the garlic with a dash of salt. Mix with a bit of yogurt to make a paste, and add the rest of the yogurt to the paste and blend. Add the mint and stir to mix everything well.

Drain the cucumbers, pat them dry and add them to the yogurt. Sprinkle with pepper. If not serving immediately, refrigerate the soup to keep it chilled.

Yield: 4 to 6 servings.

VARIATIONS

The Persians substitute fresh dill for the mint, and add raisins (which have been soaked in water) and chopped hard-boiled eggs.

Add finely diced cold cooked potatoes to the soup.

See also Creamed Cucumber Soup I and II (pages 40 and 41).

Creamed Cucumber Soup I

2 medium cucumbers, about 1½ pounds
4 tablespoons butter
1 tablespoon minced shallots or scallions
¼ cup flour
2 cups hot chicken stock
½ teaspoon salt (or to taste)
Pepper to taste (preferably white)
2 cups yogurt
Minced parsley or dill

Peel the cucumbers, split them lengthwise and scoop out the seeds with the tip of a spoon. Place the cucumbers in boiling salted water to cover, and simmer for about 3 minutes. Drain and cube them. There should be about 3 cups.

In a heavy pan, melt the butter and add the shallots or scallions. Cook over moderate heat for a few minutes until they are soft, but not brown. Add the flour and cook for a few minutes, blending flour and butter well with a spoon. Remove the pan from the heat and add the hot stock all at once, beating it in with a wire whisk.

Return the pan to the heat and cook the mixture over moderate heat, stirring, until hot and smooth. Add the cucumbers, salt and pepper, and simmer the mixture for about 15 minutes. Remove from heat and puree the mixture in a blender or by forcing it through a sieve.

If serving soup hot, return the mixture to the pan, add the yogurt and stir to blend thoroughly. Heat, but do not let it come to a boil.

If serving soup cold, let it cool slightly, stir in the yogurt and mix well. Refrigerate for several hours.

Garnish with minced parsley or dill.

Yield: 4 to 6 servings.

Creamed Cucumber Soup II

2 tablespoons butter
¼ cup chopped onion
2 medium or 3 small cucumbers,
    peeled and diced (about 2 cups)
1 small raw potato, diced
1 cup watercress leaves, lightly packed
2 cups chicken broth
1 bay leaf
½ teaspoon salt
Pepper to taste
¼ to ½ teaspoon dry mustard
Pinch of dried dill
2 cups plain yogurt
Chopped chives or scallion stems

In a heavy pan, melt the butter and sauté the onion over low heat for a few minutes, until soft and translucent but not brown. Add the remaining ingredients except the yogurt and chopped chives or scallion stems, and bring the mixture to a boil. Lower the heat and simmer the soup for about 15 minutes or until the potato is tender.

Puree the mixture in a blender or force it through a sieve. Taste and adjust the seasonings.

If serving soup hot, return the mixture to the pan and reheat it. Just before serving, add the yogurt and heat it briefly, stirring. Do not let it boil. Garnish with chopped chives or scallion stems and some croutons.

If you are serving the soup cold, allow it to cool after you have pureed it. Add the yogurt, stirring to blend well. Refrigerate for several hours. Garnish with chopped chives or scallion stems.

Yield: 4 to 6 servings.

Cold Eggplant Soup

1/3 cup vegetable or olive oil
1 medium eggplant (about 1 pound), peeled
    and cubed
1 medium-size sweet red or green pepper, seeded
    and coarsely chopped
½ cup water or chicken stock
1 clove garlic
Salt and pepper to taste
½ teaspoon crushed dried mint, or
    1 tablespoon chopped fresh mint
1 teaspoon lemon juice
½ teaspoon Worcestershire
Few drops tabasco
3 to 4 cups yogurt
2 tablespoons minced parsley, chives or
    scallion stems

In a heavy pan, heat the oil and add the cubed eggplant and chopped pepper. Cook over low heat, turning the pieces with a spoon to coat them lightly with the oil. Cover the pan and let the eggplant and pepper cook for a minute over low heat. Add the water or stock, the garlic, salt and pepper, and simmer for about 15 minutes. If you are using dried mint, add it for the last 5 minutes of cooking.

Puree the contents of the pan with the fresh mint, lemon juice, Worcestershire and tabasco, using blender. Taste and adjust seasonings.

Add 3 cups of the yogurt and blend briefly. Refrigerate for at least 4 hours. Before serving, add as much of the remaining yogurt as you like, depending on the consistency you want. Serve very cold, garnished with minced parsley, chives or scallion stems.

Yield: 6 servings.

Cold Mongole Soup

2 tablespoons butter
1 stalk celery, chopped
1 small onion, minced
1 carrot, scraped and chopped
1 tablespoon curry powder (or to taste)
½ cup water
1 bay leaf
One 18-ounce can tomato juice
One 10½-ounce can condensed split pea or
    green pea soup
Salt and pepper to taste
2 cups yogurt

In a heavy pan, melt the butter and add the celery, onion and carrot. Cook over low heat for about 5 minutes. Add the curry powder and stir to blend well. Cook for about 2 or 3 minutes, stirring. Add the water and bay leaf. Add the tomato juice, pea soup, and salt and pepper, using a wire whisk to blend. When the soup is smooth and blended, cover and let simmer for about 30 minutes. Taste and adjust seasonings, and let the soup cool slightly. Remove bay leaf.

Puree the soup in a blender. Add the yogurt and blend briefly. Taste and adjust seasonings. Refrigerate for several hours. Serve very cold.

Yield: 4 to 6 servings.

Hungarian Mushroom Soup

3 tablespoons butter
1 clove garlic, minced
2 to 3 tablespoons minced onion
¾ pound mushrooms, chopped or sliced
2 tablespoons flour
1 teaspoon salt
1 teaspoon sweet Hungarian paprika
4 cups hot chicken stock
2/3 cup thick yogurt**
1 tablespoon minced parsley (preferably flat-leaf)

In a heavy pan, melt the butter over low heat and sauté the garlic, onion and mushrooms for about 6 or 7 minutes. Stir in the flour, salt and paprika, and blend well. Add a cup of the chicken stock and beat it with a wire whisk until blended and smooth. Continue adding the rest of the stock, blending it in. Bring the soup just to the boil. Taste and adjust seasonings.

Beat the thick yogurt lightly with a fork. Ladle the soup into soup cups and add 2 tablespoons thick yogurt to each cup. Garnish with a sprinkling of minced parsley.

Yield: 6 servings.

**See page 16.

Cream of Pea with Watercress Soup

Two 10-ounce packages frozen peas
1 cup watercress leaves, lightly packed
2 cups chicken broth
Salt and pepper to taste
2 cups yogurt

Cook the peas until they are barely tender. Drain them and set aside.

Wash the watercress well, cutting off and discarding the coarse stems. Place about 2/3 of the watercress in a pan with the chicken broth (save the rest of the cress for a garnish). Simmer for about 15 minutes. Add the peas, salt and pepper to the pan, remove the pan from the heat and let the mixture cool. Taste and adjust seasonings.

Puree the mixture in a blender. If you are serving it hot, return it to the pan and reheat gently. Add the yogurt and cook briefly, but do not let it boil.

If you are serving it cold, let it cook before pureeing in the blender with the yogurt. Refrigerate for several hours. Stir gently before serving. Garnish each soup bowl with some of the reserved watercress leaves.

Yield: 4 to 6 servings.

Cold Minted Split Pea Soup

1 pound dried green split peas
6 cups chicken stock
1 cup chopped onion
½ cup chopped celery
1 cup finely chopped mint leaves, packed
1 bay leaf
Salt to taste
White pepper to taste
1 cup yogurt
6 mint sprigs

Wash the peas thoroughly under cold water. In a large heavy pot, combine the peas and stock with the onion, celery, mint, bay leaf, salt and pepper. Bring to a rolling boil, partially cover the pot and lower the heat. Simmer for 1½ to 2 hours, stirring occasionally. The peas should be thoroughly cooked and very soft.

Remove the bay leaf and puree the soup in a food mill (fine disk) or a blender. Stir in ½ cup of the yogurt; taste and adjust seasonings. Remember, the soup will be served chilled, so overseason slightly. Cover the soup and chill it thoroughly for several hours or overnight.

When ready to serve the soup (which will have thickened quite a bit) thin it with the remaining ½ cup (or more) of yogurt. Taste and adjust seasonings. Garnish each serving with a sprig of mint.

Yield: 6 servings.

Peanut Soup

4 tablespoons butter
1 small onion, chopped
2 stalks celery, chopped
2 tablespoons flour
1 cup creamy peanut butter
4 cups chicken or beef broth
1 tablespoon lemon juice
Salt to taste
1 cup yogurt
¼ cup coarsely chopped peanuts

In a heavy pan, melt the butter over moderate heat and sauté the onion and celery until they are limp and wilted but not brown. Sprinkle them with the flour. Stir to blend everything together and cook for a minute or so. Add the peanut butter, stirring and blending it in. Then add the broth, lemon juice and salt. Heat thoroughly and adjust the seasoning. Add the yogurt and continue cooking over moderate heat until the soup is hot. Do not let it boil. Taste and adjust seasoning.

Serve the hot soup in individual bowls, garnished with the chopped peanuts.

Yield: 4 to 6 servings.

Note: This is a very rich and filling soup, so plan the rest of your menu with that in mind.

Pumpkin Soup

1 small onion, chopped
1 pound peeled, cubed fresh pumpkin, or
*   one 1-pound can pumpkin*
3 cups chicken broth
Salt and pepper to taste
1 cup drained yogurt**
6 slices ripe tomato
3 tablespoons finely chopped chives or
*   scallion stems*

If you are using fresh pumpkin, in a large heavy pan, combine the chopped onion with the fresh pumpkin and the broth. Bring to a boil, cover and let simmer for about 15 minutes.

If you are using canned pumpkin, let the chopped onion simmer in the chicken broth for about 10 minutes, covered, then stir in the pumpkin. Add salt and pepper and let the mixture simmer, covered, for about 5 minutes.

If you are serving the soup hot, puree the mixture in a blender or force through a sieve, and add the drained yogurt. Return it to the pan and reheat gently, stirring, but do not let it boil.

If you are serving the soup cold, let it cool. Puree the cooled soup in a blender with the yogurt. Refrigerate for several hours.

Serve in individual soup bowls and garnish each serving with a slice of tomato sprinkled with chopped chives or scallion stems.

Yield: 6 servings.

**See page 16.

Senegalese Soup

4 tablespoons butter
3 stalks celery, chopped
2 medium onions, chopped
1 tablespoon curry powder
1 tablespoon flour
6 cups chicken broth
2 medium cooking apples, peeled and chopped
Salt and pepper to taste
1 bay leaf
1 cup yogurt
1 cup cooked chicken (preferably breast meat) cut
    into julienne strips
Paprika (optional)

In a heavy pan, melt the butter over low heat and sauté the celery and onions until they are soft and limp but not brown. Add the curry powder and cook for about 3 minutes, stirring to blend. Add the flour and cook for a minute or two, stirring to blend. Add the broth, apples, salt, pepper and bay leaf. Simmer the soup for about 30 minutes, until vegetables are very soft. Taste and adjust seasonings.

Remove the bay leaf and let the soup cool. Puree in a blender until it is very smooth. Stir in the yogurt and refrigerate.

To serve, place the strips of chicken in the bottom of each soup bowl. Stir the soup well and ladle it on top of the chicken strips. If you like, sprinkle a few grains of paprika (for color) on top of each serving.

Yield: 6 to 8 servings.

Cold Cream of Tomato Soup

3 large or 4 medium tomatoes
1 medium onion, sliced
1 clove garlic
1 cup chicken broth
1 tablespoon tomato paste
2 teaspoons dried dill
½ teaspoon salt (or to taste)
¼ teaspoon pepper
½ cup diced cooked potato or cooked macaroni
1 cup drained yogurt**
Snipped fresh dill or minced parsley

Peel the tomatoes. Slice them and place in a heavy pan with the onion, garlic, broth, tomato paste, dill, salt and pepper. Cover the pan and bring the mixture to a boil over moderate heat, stirring occasionally to blend. Lower the heat and simmer for about 15 minutes. Remove the pan from the heat and allow the mixture to cool.

Puree the soup in a blender with the potato or macaroni until very smooth. Add the yogurt and blend briefly. Refrigerate for several hours before serving. Garnish each serving with a little snipped fresh dill or minced parsley.

Yield: 6 servings.

Note: Canned tomatoes (drained) may be substituted for the fresh ones in the recipe. Cooked rice can also be used as a thickening agent.

**See page 16.

Tomato Sherbet

One 15-ounce can of clam-and-tomato juice
1 cup tomato juice
1 tablespoon lemon juice
½ teaspoon Worcestershire (or to taste)
½ teaspoon salt (or to taste)
¼ teaspoon pepper
½ teaspoon curry powder (or to taste—optional)
Few drops tabasco
1 to 2 cups yogurt
Lemon slices

Mix all ingredients except the yogurt and lemon slices and place in an ice cube tray in your freezer so that it will freeze in cube form. *Note:* If you have a tray that freezes slices, rather than cubes, it is preferable.

Puree the cubes either before they are completely frozen or let frozen ones thaw slightly. Puree in a blender or food processor with 1 cup yogurt, and serve as a sherbet, garnishing each serving with a lemon slice.

Or puree the cubes with 2 cups of yogurt and serve as a very thick, cold spicy soup.

Yield: 4 to 6 servings.

Note: Store the frozen cubes in a plastic bag in your freezing compartment and you will have a quick last-minute soup for an extra-hot night or for an unexpected guest.

Creamed Vegetable Soup

3 tablespoons butter
2 to 3 cups cooked vegetables (beans, carrots,
*   peas, cabbage, Brussels sprouts, spinach, etc.)*
2 to 3 cups chicken or beef broth or vegetable stock
½ teaspoon salt (or to taste)
¼ teaspoon crushed dried tarragon
Pinch of nutmeg
Pepper to taste
1 cup yogurt
Minced parsley or chives

In a heavy pan, melt the butter over low heat and toss the vegetables to coat them lightly. Cook them for about 3 minutes, stirring. Add the broth, salt, tarragon, nutmeg and pepper, and cook for about 5 minutes. Cool slightly. Taste and adjust seasonings.

Puree the mixture in a blender or food mill, or force through a sieve.

If serving soup hot, return to the pan to reheat and stir in the yogurt. Reheat gently, but do not let it boil.

If serving soup cold, add the yogurt to the pureed mixture and blend briefly or stir in. Refrigerate for an hour or more. Garnish with minced parsley or chives.

Yield: 4 to 6 servings.

Cold Watercress Soup

1 cup watercress, packed leaves
2 tablespoons vegetable oil
1 small onion, chopped
1½ teaspoons salt
1 tablespoon flour
2 cups chicken broth
¼ teaspoon pepper
½ teaspoon crushed dried dill
½ teaspoon crushed dried tarragon
Few drops Worcestershire
1 teaspoon lemon juice
2 cups yogurt

Heat the oil in a heavy pan, add the onion and cook over moderate heat until the onion is soft and wilted but not brown. Add the watercress, reserving a few leaves for garnish. Sprinkle on the salt and toss well to mix. Cook for about 5 minutes, stirring occasionally, or until the cress is wilted. Sprinkle on the flour, mix it in well and cook for about 2 or 3 minutes. Add the chicken broth, blending it thoroughly with a wire whisk, and simmer for about 5 minutes. Add the pepper, dill and tarragon and simmer for about 10 minutes. Taste and adjust seasonings.

Let the soup cool, add the Worcestershire, lemon juice, and puree in a blender. Add half the yogurt and blend briefly. Add the balance of the yogurt and blend briefly. Refrigerate for several hours before serving. Garnish each bowl with a few watercress leaves.

Yield: 4 servings.

Cold Zucchini Soup

4 large zucchini (about 2½ pounds)
4 tablespoons butter
1 large onion, chopped
3 cups chicken stock
1 clove garlic, minced
¼ teaspoon dried chervil
Salt and pepper to taste
2 cups yogurt
3 tablespoons minced chives or
    scallion stems

Scrub the zucchini but do not peel; cut into chunks.

In a heavy pan, melt the butter over moderate heat and cook the onion until soft but not brown. Add the zucchini pieces and let them cook for a few minutes. Add the chicken stock, garlic, chervil, salt and pepper, and simmer for about 15 minutes. The zucchini should just be soft. Remove from heat and let cool slightly. Taste and adjust the seasonings.

Puree the cooled mixture in a blender. Add the yogurt and blend briefly. Refrigerate for several hours. Serve very cold, garnished with the minced chives or scallion stems.

Yield: 6 to 8 servings.

Fish and Seafood

Baked Fish Filets and Tomatoes

*1½ cups tomatoes, peeled, seeded, juiced and very
    coarsely cut up, or one 17-ounce can Italian
    plum tomatoes, drained and coarsely cut up*
Salt and pepper to taste
½ cup yogurt cheese**
2 tablespoons yogurt
*2 tablespoons fresh dill, or
    1 teaspoon dried dill*
1½ to 2 pounds fish filets, cut into serving pieces

Preheat the oven to 450°.

Place the tomatoes in a shallow, lightly buttered baking dish and sprinkle them with salt and pepper.

Mash the yogurt cheese with the yogurt and mix well with the dill. Sprinkle the fish with salt and pepper and spread one side of the filets with half of the yogurt-and-dill mixture. Place the fish, sauce side down, on the tomatoes. Spread the remainder of the sauce on the top of the fish.

Place the dish in the lower third of the oven and bake until fish is pierced easily with a fork, about 10 minutes per inch of thickness.

Serve with rice or potatoes and a green vegetable, such as peas, broccoli or string beans.

Yield: 4 servings.

**See page 16.

Baked Fish Filets and Mushrooms

3 or 4 medium potatoes (about 1 pound)
¼ pound mushrooms
2 tablespoons butter
1 small onion, thinly sliced
¼ cup dry white wine or dry vermouth
Salt and pepper to taste
1 tablespoon flour
1 cup yogurt
1½ to 2 pounds fish filets, cut into serving pieces
Bread crumbs
2 tablespoons minced parsley

Peel and boil the potatoes in boiling salted water for about 30 minutes, until they are just soft. While the potatoes are cooking, wipe the mushrooms with a damp cloth or paper towel and slice them thinly (there should be about 1 cup).

In a heavy pan, melt 1 tablespoon of the butter and add the onion slices. Cook over low heat until soft and limp but not brown. Remove onion from the pan and set aside. In the same pan, toss the sliced mushrooms and sauté them for a minute or so. Return the onions to the pan, add the wine or vermouth and simmer for about 4 or 5 minutes.

Preheat the oven to 450°.

Lightly butter a shallow baking dish. When the potatoes are cooked, slice them thinly and place them in the baking dish. Sprinkle them with salt and pepper and dot them with the remaining butter. Reserving the pan juices, remove the mushrooms and onion from the pan with a slotted spoon and spread them over the potatoes. Beat the flour into the yogurt and place in a small saucepan, stirring with a wire whisk until the mixture comes to a gentle boil. Allow the sauce to bubble for about a minute and then beat in the mushroom juices with a whisk. Add salt and pepper.

Place the fish filets on top of the mushrooms and onion, sprinkling them with a little salt and pepper. Cover the fish with the sauce and sprinkle with the bread crumbs (the bread crumbs serve a cosmetic purpose, as the mushroom juices add flavor but tend to color the sauce a somewhat unappetizing beige).

Bake until fish is pierced easily with a fork, about 10 minutes per inch of thickness. Garnish with minced parsley.

Serve with chopped spinach or coarsely shredded zucchini sautéed in a little butter, and a mixed green salad.

Yield: 4 servings.

Baked Fish Filets with Celery Root

3 or 4 medium potatoes (about 1 pound)
1 large or 2 medium celery roots (about 1 pound)
Salt and pepper to taste
2 tablespoons butter
1½ cups thick yogurt**
1½ to 2 pounds fish filets, cut into serving pieces
Paprika

Peel the potatoes and drop them into a bowl of cold water. Peel the celery root and drop it into the same bowl.

In a large quantity of boiling salted water, boil the potatoes for about 15 minutes. Add the celery root to the same pot and boil the vegetables for about 15 to 20 minutes longer, or until the potatoes are just soft and the celery root is just tender. Drain and slice them thinly (there should be about 2 cups of each).

Preheat the oven to 450°.

Lightly butter a shallow ovenproof dish and alternately layer the potato and celery root slices, sprinkling with salt and pepper and dotting the layers with bits of butter. Spread half the thick yogurt on the vegetables. Arrange the fish filets on top, sprinkle with salt and pepper and top with the rest of the thick yogurt.

Bake until fish is easily pierced with a fork, about 10 minutes per inch of thickness. Sprinkle with a bit of paprika (for color) before serving.

A green vegetable and carrots tossed with parsley would be nice with this.

Yield: 4 to 6 servings.

**See page 16.

Cauliflower and Crabmeat

1 large head cauliflower, about 2 pounds
Two 6-ounce packages frozen crabmeat, thawed, or
    two 6½-ounce cans crabmeat
2 tablespoons butter
2 tablespoons flour
1 teaspoon paprika
¼ cup crab liquid or fish stock   (see Note)
1 cup yogurt
*¼ cup yogurt cream**
Salt and fresh ground pepper to taste
Few drops tabasco
Few drops lemon juice
2 tablespoons minced parsley

Trim the cauliflower of its green leaves and cut off part of the stem (save the trimmings for soup or Green Vegetable Dip—page 20). Break the cauliflower into florets and cook in boiling salted water until it is barely tender. Do not overcook. While it is cooking, make the sauce.

Drain the crabmeat, if necessary, reserving the liquid. Pick over crabmeat and discard membranes.

In a heavy pan, melt the butter. Add the flour and paprika and stir to blend thoroughly. When blended, add the crab liquid or fish stock and yogurt, stirring briskly with a wire whisk. Add the yogurt cream and season with salt, pepper, tabasco and lemon juice. Cook over moderate heat until the sauce is smooth and bubbling. Add the crabmeat and let it come just to a boil.

Drain the cauliflower florets and place on a warmed platter. Pour the crab and sauce over the cauliflower and sprinkle with the parsley.

Yield: 4 to 6 servings.

Note: If necessary, you can stretch the crab liquid to ¼ cup by adding dry white wine or dry vermouth. Fish stock can also be made by diluting bottled clam juice with an equal amount of water and simmering it with a few parsley stems for about 20 minutes. The stock will be quite salty, so adjust your seasonings accordingly.

**See page 16.

Crabmeat and Mushrooms

1 pound fresh, two 6-ounce packages frozen, or
*   two 6½-ounce cans crabmeat*
3 tablespoons butter
¼ pound mushrooms, sliced
2 tablespoons flour
½ teaspoon dry mustard
¼ teaspoon dried tarragon
¼ teaspoon paprika
Salt and pepper to taste
1 cup yogurt
*¼ cup yogurt cream***
Bread crumbs
1 tablespoon butter

Preheat the oven to 350°.

Drain the crabmeat if necessary.

Pick over the crabmeat, remove the membranes and set the crab-meat aside.

In a heavy pan, melt 1 tablespoon of the butter and sauté the mushrooms for about 5 or 6 minutes over moderate heat. Remove the mushrooms and their juices and set aside.

Melt 2 tablespoons butter in the pan, blend in the flour and cook, stirring, for a couple of minutes. Add the seasonings and gradually add the yogurt and yogurt cream, stirring and cooking over low heat until the sauce is smooth and thick and starting to bubble. Add the crabmeat and mushrooms. Taste and adjust seasonings.

Turn mixture into 4 individual baking dishes or one large shallow baking dish. Sprinkle bread crumbs on top and dot with 1 table-spoon butter, cut into small bits.

Bake for about 15 minutes, then put under the broiler for a few minutes to brown.

Serve with wild or white rice or cooked cracked wheat (bulghour). Possible vegetable accompaniments might include string beans with sliced water chestnuts, or cucumber strips, boiled in salted water for about 3 minutes and tossed with minced parsley and dill and a small amount of butter.

Yield: 4 servings.

**See page 16.

Baked Salmon Steaks

½ teaspoon mustard
1 tablespoon lemon juice
2 cups thick yogurt**
1 teaspoon capers
Salt
4 salmon steaks (1½ to 2 pounds)
Pepper

Preheat the oven to 450°.

Stir the mustard in the lemon juice to dissolve, and beat this into the thick yogurt. Stir in the capers. Taste and add salt if necessary.

Place the salmon steaks in a shallow buttered casserole, sprinkle with a little salt and pepper and pour the sauce over the fish.

Bake until fish is pierced easily with a fork, about 10 minutes per inch of thickness.

Serve with buttered rice tossed with minced parsley or tiny new potatoes (boiled or steamed) tossed with butter and parsley. Chopped spinach, broccoli or peas would go nicely with this.

Yield: 4 servings.

VARIATIONS

Substitute swordfish or halibut steaks for the salmon.

**See page 16.

Tuna Florentine

2 pounds fresh spinach, or
two 10-ounce packages frozen spinach
3 tablespoons butter
3 tablespoons flour
1 cup boiling chicken broth
1 cup drained yogurt**
1 tablespoon lemon juice (or to taste)
Salt and pepper to taste
Two 7-ounce cans tuna (preferably water-pack),
drained and flaked
Buttered bread crumbs

Cook the spinach until it is tender, drain it thoroughly and chop it. Set it aside.

Preheat the oven to 350°.

In a saucepan, melt the butter over moderate heat and blend in the flour, letting them cook together for a minute or two. Remove the pan from the heat. Add the boiling chicken broth. Stir with a wire whisk until blended and smooth and return the pan to the heat. When the sauce is thickened and bubbling, lower the heat, add the yogurt, stirring to blend it in thoroughly. Add the lemon juice, salt and pepper, and cook for a few minutes, until sauce is gently bubbling.

Spread the spinach in a lightly buttered shallow baking dish and mix in half of the sauce. Spread the tuna over the spinach and pour on the rest of the sauce. Top with the buttered bread crumbs and bake for about 15 to 20 minutes.

Serve with rice or noodles. Cherry tomatoes could be baked in the oven along with the tuna: Roll them around in a baking dish with a little softened butter and sprinkle with salt, pepper and chopped parsley before baking them.

Yield: 4 servings.

**See page 16.

Tuna Loaf

2 tablespoons butter
¼ cup finely chopped onion
¼ cup finely chopped celery
1½ teaspoons curry powder
½ cup thick yogurt**
½ cup bread crumbs
Salt and pepper to taste
1 egg, beaten
Two 7-ounce cans tuna, well drained
Lemon juice (optional)

Preheat the oven to 350°.

In a saucepan, melt the butter and cook the onion and celery until barely soft. Add the curry powder, blend well and cook over low heat for about 2 minutes. Add the thick yogurt, stirring to blend, and the bread crumbs, salt and pepper. Remove the pan from the heat, and blend in the beaten egg and tuna. Add the lemon juice, taste, and adjust seasonings.

Turn the mixture into a greased loaf pan and bake until lightly browned for about 40 minutes.

Unmold and serve with Dill Sauce (see page 156). Grilled tomato halves or baked cherry tomatoes would go well with this. A spinach and sliced mushroom salad would also be nice.

Yield: 4 to 6 servings.

**See page 16.

Salmon Loaf

2 cups cooked salmon, or one
*   16-ounce can salmon*
2 tablespoons butter
¼ cup minced onion
¼ cup finely chopped celery
¼ cup thick yogurt**
¾ cup bread crumbs
1 egg, separated
Few drops tabasco
2 tablespoons fresh dill, or
*   1 teaspoon dried dill*
¼ cup finely chopped parsley
Salt and pepper to taste
Lemon juice to taste

Preheat the oven to 350°.

Drain the salmon, if necessary, and break it up in a bowl with a fork. If using canned salmon, remove bones and skin.

In a saucepan, melt the butter over low heat and cook the onion and celery until barely tender. Add the thick yogurt and bread crumbs and stir thoroughly. Remove the pan from the heat and let it stand for a few minutes.

Beat the egg yolk briefly with the tabasco, and add to the salmon. Add the onion-celery-bread crumb mixture. Add the dill, parsley, salt and pepper, and blend all the ingredients thoroughly. Taste and add a few drops of lemon juice. Beat the egg white until it is stiff, and fold it in.

Turn the mixture into a greased loaf pan and bake until lightly browned for about 35 to 40 minutes.

Unmold and serve with Dill Sauce (see page 163).

Yield: 4 to 6 servings.

**See page 16.

Shrimp with Rice

1½ tablespoons butter
¼ cup minced onion, shallots or scallion heads
1 cup raw rice
½ teaspoon salt
Tabasco
1½ cups boiling water
1 lb. cooked and cleaned medium shrimp, fresh or frozen
    (if frozen, thawed and thoroughly dried)
2 cups drained yogurt**
2 tablespoons tomato paste
1 tablespoon minced fresh dill or
    1½ teaspoons dried dill
1 or 2 tablespoons mayonnaise (optional)
Parsley, minced

In a heavy pan, melt the butter over moderate heat and saute the minced onion until it is limp but not brown. Add the rice and stir until the grains are coated. Add the salt and a drop or two of tabasco. Add the boiling water. When the rice has returned to the boil, cover the pan and lower the heat. Cook the rice for exactly 17 minutes without removing the cover. (The rice can also be baked in a preheated oven for the same amount of time.)

In another pan, blend the yogurt and tomato paste over low heat. Add the dill and a dash of tabasco. Add salt to taste. For extra richness, stir in the optional mayonnaise. Do not let the sauce boil. Add the shrimp and warm gently in the sauce shortly before the rice is ready.

Toss the rice with the parsley. Serve with the shrimp and rice mixed together, with the sauce over the rice or on the side.

Yield: 4 to 6 servings.

**See page 16.

Meat and Poultry

Meat Loaf

2 pounds ground beef
½ pound ground veal
½ pound ground pork (see Note)
2 cloves garlic, minced
1 medium onion, finely chopped
½ cup bread crumbs
1 egg, beaten with ½ cup thick yogurt**
1 teaspoon salt
1 teaspoon freshly ground pepper
½ teaspoon crushed dried thyme
6 slices bacon

Preheat the oven to 325°.

Mix together all the ingredients except the bacon, making sure that they are completely blended. Form the mixture into a loaf shape.

Using either a loaf pan or a rectangular ovenproof baking dish, place 4 strips of the bacon on the bottom of the pan and place the meat loaf on them. Place the 2 remaining strips of bacon on top of the meat loaf and bake, basting every 15 minutes, for about 1½ hours. Allow the meat loaf to rest for 15 minutes before slicing it.

Serve with baked stuffed potatoes, carrots and a tossed salad.

Yield: 6 to 8 servings.

Note: You can eliminate veal and use 1 pound ground pork.

For a cold supper, cook the meat loaf a day in advance and refrigerate it. The next day, allow it to come to room temperature, then slice and garnish with sliced tomatoes and watercress.

**See page 16.

Beef with Mustard Sauce

1 tablespoon butter or oil
½ cup minced onion
¼ pound mushrooms, sliced
1 pound thin cubed beefsteaks or
    sandwich steaks cut into strips 3/8 inch wide
½ cup dry white wine or dry vermouth
1 tablespoon Dijon-type mustard
1 teaspoon paprika
½ teaspoon salt
¼ teaspoon pepper
1 cup thick yogurt**

In a large heavy skillet, heat the butter or oil, and saute the onion over moderate heat for about 5 minutes, until tender but not brown. Add the sliced mushrooms to the pan and cook them gently for about 5 minutes. Add the beef strips and sauté with the onions and mushrooms for about 2 or 3 minutes, turning the strips occasionally.

In a small bowl, combine the wine or vermouth, mustard and seasonings, stirring until well blended. Add this mixture to the pan. Bring to a boil, then lower the heat and simmer for about 2 or 3 minutes, stirring occasionally. Add the thick yogurt. Heat, but do not allow it to boil. Taste and adjust seasonings.

Serve with buttered noodles tossed with poppy seeds or with rice mixed lightly with melted butter and chopped parsley. Cooked carrots and celery, or shredded cooked zucchini would go well with this.

Yield: 4 servings.

**See page 16.

Meatballs

1 pound finely ground beef or lamb,
  or a combination of both
2 tablespoons minced shallots, or
  1 tablespoon minced onion
½ teaspoon salt (or to taste)
¼ teaspoon pepper
1/8 teaspoon nutmeg
½ cup bread crumbs
¼ cup yogurt cheese**
2 tablespoons red currant jelly
4 tablespoons butter or oil, or a
  mixture of both
½ cup beef bouillon
1 tablespoon Madeira, sherry or Marsala
Few drops tabasco
2 tablespoons yogurt cream** (optional)

Mix together the meat, shallots or onion, salt, pepper and nutmeg. Add the bread crumbs, yogurt cheese and jelly. Blend thoroughly with your fingertips and form into 8 small meatballs.

In a large heavy skillet, melt the butter or oil over moderately high heat and quickly brown the meatballs on all sides. Add the bouillon, wine and tabasco, and cook the meatballs for about 5 minutes (or longer if you prefer them well done), basting them with the pan juices.

Remove the meatballs from the pan and place them on a warm platter. Raise the heat and quickly reduce the pan juices. Add the yogurt cream, stir to blend and pour the juices over the meatballs.

Serve with baked stuffed potatoes or Potato and Celery Root au Gratin (see page 121). Cherry tomatoes, tossed with a little butter and chopped parsley and baked for about 15 minutes, would also go well, along with a mixed green salad or a cooked green vegetable.

Yield: 4 servings.

**See page 16.

Spicy Hamburgers

2 tablespoons seedless raisins
1 cup thick yogurt**
2 tablespoons powdered coriander
½ teaspoon powdered cardamom
1 teaspoon cayenne pepper
1 teaspoon salt
1 to 2 tablespoons water
1½ pounds lean ground beef
2 tablespoons butter or oil, or
*   a combination of both*
1 medium onion, thinly sliced
1 teaspoon cornstarch mixed with
*   1 teaspoon water*

Stir the raisins into the thick yogurt and set them aside for about 30 minutes.

Mix the coriander, cardamom, cayenne and salt with enough water to make a smooth paste, which should spread easily but not be too watery.

Form the beef into 4 patties and spread both sides of them with the spice paste.

In a large heavy skillet, heat the butter or oil and cook the onion over moderate heat until soft and translucent but not brown. Push the onion to one side and add the meat patties to the pan. Brown them very quickly on one side, then turn them and brown the other side.

Lower the heat and add a tablespoon of the yogurt-and-raisin mixture to the pan, stirring to blend. Continue cooking, turning the meat and adding tablespoons of the yogurt-and-raisin mixture gradually until the meat is cooked to your preference. This should take about 5 minutes for pink hamburgers, longer for well-done ones. Remove the hamburgers from the pan to a warm serving platter.

Add the cornstarch-and-water mixture to the pan, stirring to blend thoroughly. Raise the heat and cook the sauce for a minute or two before pouring it over the hamburgers.

Serve with boiled rice and sliced cucumbers tossed with vinegar, oil and a little mint.

Yield: 4 servings.

**See page 16.

Creamed Chipped Beef

4 tablespoons butter or margarine
2 tablespoons minced onion
¼ pound mushrooms, sliced
One 2½-ounce jar dried chipped beef,
*   rinsed in water and drained*
¼ cup flour
2 cups yogurt
Pepper to taste
Pinch of nutmeg (or to taste)
Minced parsley

In a large heavy skillet, heat the butter or margarine until foamy. Add the onion and cook over moderate heat for a few minutes until soft and limp but not brown. Add the mushrooms and sauté them gently for about 5 minutes. Add the chipped beef, stirring it to mix with the onion and mushrooms. With a slotted spoon, remove the beef, onion and mushrooms to a side dish.

Add the flour to the pan, stirring it to blend with the butter and pan juices. Let this cook for a minute or two. Add the yogurt gradually, stirring until the sauce is smooth and thick.

Return the beef, onion and mushrooms to the pan. Add the pepper and nutmeg. Cook for a few minutes longer, until sauce is hot and bubbling. Sprinkle with minced parsley.

Serve with baked potatoes, mashed potatoes, potatoes pureed with cooked celery root, rice or pasta. A nice accompaniment would be hot sliced beets or cold pickled beets.

Yield: 4 servings.

Veal Stew

2 pounds boneless veal (shoulder or leg)
4 tablespoons butter
2 tablespoons oil
1 small onion, finely chopped
1 clove garlic, minced
1 cup canned peeled Italian
    plum tomatoes, well drained
3 tablespoons flour
1 tablespoon tomato paste
1 cup hot beef stock or bouillon
½ cup thick yogurt**
1 bay leaf
½ teaspoon salt (or to taste)
Freshly ground pepper to taste

Cut the veal into 2-inch cubes and dry them thoroughly between paper towels.

In a large heavy pan, heat the butter and oil until hot and foamy. Add the veal cubes and brown them on all sides over high heat (you may have to do this in 2 steps). As the cubes are browned, remove them from the pan to a side dish.

When all the meat is browned, lower the heat, add the onion and garlic to the pan and cook them for about 3 or 4 minutes, until they are tender and limp but not brown. Add the tomatoes to the pan, breaking them up with the edge of a spoon. Cook for about 3 minutes, then remove the pan from the heat. Stir in the flour and tomato paste, blending well.

Return the pan to the heat and add the stock or bouillon, stirring until the mixture comes to a boil. Boil for a minute or two. Return the veal to the pan and lower the heat. Add the thick yogurt, stirring gently but thoroughly to blend. Add the bay leaf, salt and pepper, and cook over low heat for about 40 minutes or until the veal is tender. Remove the bay leaf.

Serve with noodles or other pasta or rice, and a salad of spinach and sliced raw mushrooms.

Yield: 4 to 6 servings.

**See page 16.

Lamb Stroganoff

1½ pounds boneless lean lamb
(preferably from the leg)
2 tablespoons yogurt
4 tablespoons butter or oil, or
a combination of both
1 large onion, minced
¼ pound mushrooms, sliced
2 tablespoons flour
Salt and pepper to taste
*1 cup thick yogurt***

Cut the lamb into thin strips about 2 inches long and ½ inch wide. Toss the lamb strips with the yogurt to marinate for about an hour. Set aside.

In a large heavy pan, heat 2 tablespoons of the butter or oil and cook the onion over moderate heat until soft and golden. Remove the onion from the pan with a slotted spoon and set aside. Add the sliced mushrooms to the pan and cook for about 5 minutes, shaking the pan occasionally. Remove the mushrooms and their juices from the pan and add them to the onion. Remove the pan from the heat.

Remove the lamb strips from the yogurt and wipe them with a paper towel. Dip them in the flour and turn them so they are lightly covered with flour on all sides.

Return the pan to the heat and add the remaining 2 tablespoons of butter or oil; when it is hot, add the lamb strips. Cook them for about 3 minutes over moderately high heat, shaking the pan to turn the meat strips (chopsticks or wooden tongs are useful here). Lower the heat to moderate, add the mushrooms and onion to the pan and sprinkle with salt and pepper. Cook for about 3 or 4 minutes and add the thick yogurt. Mix gently and cook just long enough to heat the yogurt, but do not allow it to boil.

Serve with buttered noodles or rice. Buttered carrots or boiled sliced beets would go nicely.

Yield: 4 servings.

**See page 16.

Lamb Curry

4 tablespoons clarified butter or oil
2 medium onions, chopped
1 medium apple, peeled and chopped
2 cloves garlic
1½ tablespoons curry powder (or to taste)
1 tablespoon freshly grated ginger, or
*   1 teaspoon powdered ginger*
1 tablespoon tomato paste
1 teaspoon grated lemon rind
Pinch of cayenne pepper (optional)
Salt to taste
*1 cup drained yogurt***
1 pound boneless lamb (shoulder),
*   cut into 2-inch cubes*

In a heavy pan, heat 2 tablespoons of the butter or oil and add the onions, apple and garlic. Sauté them over low heat until the onion and apple are tender. Remove the garlic and discard. Add the curry powder, stirring to blend well, and cook for a minute or two. Add the ginger, tomato paste, lemon rind, cayenne, salt and drained yogurt. Stir this mixture gently but thoroughly and remove the pan from the heat while browning the lamb.

In another pan, heat the remaining 2 tablespoons of butter or oil and add the lamb. Brown the cubes on all sides over moderately high heat and transfer them to the curry sauce. Simmer over low heat until the lamb is tender, about 30 minutes.

Serve over hot rice with accompanying dishes of chutney, minted sliced cucumbers, peanuts, banana slices, raisins soaked in whiskey. Other accompaniments might be chopped green peppers and fried zucchini strips. Serve a bowl of thick yogurt** on the side.

Yield: 4 servings.

**See page 16.

Curried Lamburgers

1½ pounds ground lean lamb
*¼ cup yogurt cheese***
2 tablespoons minced shallots, or
    1½ teaspoons minced onion
2 teaspoons curry powder (or to taste)
½ teaspoon salt
1/8 teaspoon cinnamon
Pinch of ground cloves
Flour for dredging (See Note)
2 tablespoons butter or oil, or
    a combination of both
Watercress or parsley

Mix the lamb with the yogurt cheese, shallots or onions, and spices, and form into 4 flattened patties. Dredge the patties lightly in flour.

In a large heavy pan, heat the butter or oil and add the patties. Cook them over high heat about 2 or 3 minutes, turn them and cook them about 2 or 3 minutes more (or until done to your preference). Garnish with watercress or parsley.

Serve with grilled tomatoes, or cherry tomatoes broiled or baked briefly. Broccoli, spinach or string beans and a baked potato would also go well. Another excellent accompaniment would be sliced eggplant, broiled or sautéed.

Yield: 4 servings.

Note: These lamburgers can also be broiled. If you broil them, eliminate the flour dredging step.

**See page 16.

Pork Ragout

2 pounds boneless pork shoulder
2 tablespoons flour
2 tablespoons butter or oil
1 medium onion, chopped
Salt and pepper to taste
1½ tablespoons paprika
2 medium carrots, thinly sliced
2 stalks celery, thinly sliced
1 medium green pepper, thinly sliced
½ pound mushrooms, thinly sliced
1 tablespoon flour
1 cup yogurt
¼ cup minced parsley

Cut the pork into thin strips about 2 inches long and ½ inch wide. Dredge the strips lightly in the 2 tablespoons flour and shake off excess flour.

In a large heavy pan, heat the butter or oil and quickly brown the meat over moderately high heat. Lower the heat and add the onion, salt and pepper. Stir briefly. Sprinkle in the paprika, stirring, and cook for about 1 minute. Turn heat down very low, cover and let simmer for about 10 minutes.

Add the carrots, celery, green, pepper and tomatoes. Stir, cover and let simmer for 30 minutes.

Add the sliced mushrooms, cover the pan and cook for 5 minutes.

Beat the 1 tablespoon flour into the yogurt with a wire whisk. Add the yogurt-and-flour mixture to the stew and continue cooking over low heat until the sauce is thick and creamy. Taste and adjust seasonings. Simmer for about 5 minutes. Sprinkle the top with minced parsley before serving.

Serve with noodles or rice and a salad of mixed greens, such as escarole, romaine and chicory.

Yield: 4 to 6 servings.

Pork Cutlets

4 boned butterfly pork chops,
about 1¼ pounds
Flour for dredging
1 teaspoon crushed dried sage
1 teaspoon crushed dried rosemary
4 tablespoons butter or a
combination of butter and oil
Salt and pepper to taste
1 cup dry white wine
1 cup thick yogurt**
2 tablespoons minced parsley

Dip the pork cutlets in flour, turning them to cover both sides. Pat the flour into the cutlets and shake off the excess. Rub the herbs into both sides of the meat.

In a large heavy skillet, heat the butter until it is hot and foaming. Add cutlets and brown over moderate heat. Sprinkle them with salt and pepper and turn them to brown on the other side. When both sides are browned, pour in the wine. After a minute, lower the heat, cover the pan and let the meat simmer for about 10 minutes (more or less, depending on thickness of cutlets), until tender.

When the cutlets are cooked, remove them to a warm serving platter. Quickly reduce the pan juices, if necessary, to make about ½ cup of liquid. Stir in the thick yogurt, stirring constantly, until very hot. Pour this sauce over the meat and sprinkle with minced parsley.

Serve with artichoke bottoms filled with sautéed mushrooms, along with new potatoes rolled in chopped dill and melted butter, or rice or noodles.

Yield: 4 servings.

VARIATION

Use ½ cup wine and add 2 or 3 small peeled, chopped tomatoes (well drained if using canned ones) when adding the wine. When removing the meat from the pan, let the tomatoes remain to cook down with the pan juices before adding the yogurt.

**See page 16.

Pork Chops and Sauerkraut

4 pork chops, about 2 pounds
2 pounds sauerkraut
1 cup tomatoes, fresh or canned
Salt and pepper to taste
¼ cup dry white wine
1 teaspoon ground fennel seed
1 teaspoon paprika
*1 cup thick yogurt***

Preheat the oven to 350°.

In a heavy pan, sear the chops on both sides over high heat. Drain the sauerkraut, rinse it in cold water and squeeze it thoroughly. If using fresh tomatoes, peel them, squeeze them to remove seeds and juice and chop them coarsely. If using canned tomatoes, drain well and chop them coarsely.

Sprinkle the chops on both sides with salt and pepper and place them in the bottom of an ovenproof dish that has a cover. Place the sauerkraut on top of the chops and add the tomatoes. Pour the wine over all and sprinkle on the fennel and paprika, stirring very gently.

Cover the dish and bake for about 1 hour. Just before serving remove the chops, stir the thick yogurt into the sauerkraut mixture and place chops on top.

Serve with boiled or mashed potatoes and a mixed green salad.

Yield: 4 servings.

**See page 16.

Ham and Brussels Sprouts

Two 10-ounce packages frozen Brussels sprouts,
*   or two 1-pint boxes fresh Brussels sprouts*
1 cup diced cooked ham
3 tablespoons butter
3 tablespoons flour
Salt and pepper to taste
¼ teasoon nutmeg
1½ cups yogurt
½ cup grated sharp cheese

Preheat the oven to 350°.

Cook the Brussels sprouts until they are barely tender. Drain them thoroughly and spread them in a shallow buttered casserole. Sprinkle the diced cooked ham over them.

In a heavy pan, melt the 3 tablespoons butter, blend in the flour and cook over moderate heat, stirring for a minute or two. Add salt, pepper and nutmeg and slowly add the yogurt, stirring continuously, until the sauce is smooth and thick. Lower the heat, add the grated cheese and stir for just a moment. Remove the pan from the heat and continue to stir until the cheese is melted.

Pour the sauce over the Brussels sprouts and ham. Bake until the top is brown and bubbling, about 20 to 25 minutes.

Serve with either raw carrot and zucchini strips or a mixed green salad.

Yield: 4 servings.

Turkey Ring

4 tablespoons butter
¼ cup flour
2 cups yogurt
2 chicken bouillon cubes dissolved in
    ¼ cup dry vermouth
¼ teaspoon nutmeg
Salt and pepper to taste
2 eggs, well beaten
½ cup mayonnaise
2 cups diced cooked turkey (or chicken)
½ cup slivered blanced almonds
One 5-ounce can water chestnuts, sliced
One 5-ounce can Chinese fried noodles
Watercress for garnish

Preheat the oven to 350°.

In a large heavy pan, melt the butter. Add the flour and stir to blend thoroughly. Cook the roux for 2 or 3 minutes, over low heat, then add the yogurt, bouillon-and-vermouth mixture, nutmeg, salt and pepper. Cook, stirring continuously, until the sauce is smooth and bubbling. Taste and adjust seasonings.

Let sauce cool slightly. Add the beaten eggs, stirring them in well.

Add the mayonnaise, turkey, almonds, water chestnuts and noodles, and mix thoroughly.

Turn into a well-greased 8- to 10-cup ring mold (see Note) and bake for 50 to 60 minutes. Let stand for about 5 minutes before molding. Garnish with watercress.

Fill the center with any one of the following:

- Sliced carrots tossed with butter and chopped parsley.
- Artichoke hearts (canned or frozen), cooked and tossed lightly with butter and a little lemon juice.
- Pureed spinach.
- Sautéed sliced mushrooms—½ pound sautéed in 2 tablespoons butter for about 5 minutes, sprinkled with ¼ teaspoon salt and a few drops lemon juice. When done, add 2 or 3 table-spoons cream to the pan and continue cooking, stirring until cream has thickened slightly.

Serve the ring with a separate bowl of Mushroom Sauce (see page 162), if desired.

Yield: 6 to 8 servings.

Note: If you do not have a ring mold, use a loaf pan instead. After unmolding, garnish with watercress and serve vegetables and sauce separately. This can also be baked in a large oval or rectangular ovenproof serving dish and served directly from the dish.

Chicken and Butterflies

3 large or 2 small whole chicken breasts,
*   skinned and boned*
Salt and pepper to taste
½ cup flour
8 ounces butterfly-shaped pasta (called bows)
3 or 4 tablespoons clarified butter or oil
1 tablespoon butter, softened
1 cup thick yogurt** at room temperature
Black pepper
Freshly grated Parmesan cheese

Cut the chicken into strips about 2 inches long and 3/8 inches wide—about the size of a thin little finger. Season the strips on both sides with salt and pepper and dip them in the flour, turning them so they are completely covered. Shake off the excess flour.

Place the pasta in a large quantity of boiling salted water and cook according to package directions.

While the pasta is cooking, heat the clarified butter or oil in a large heavy skillet over moderately high heat (do not let it brown or smoke). Add the chicken strips to the pan and toss and turn them (wooden tongs or chopsticks are useful here). Cook the chicken for about 3 minutes, turning and tossing until done (they should feel springy when touched).

Drain the pasta and place it in a large warm serving bowl or on a warm serving platter. Immediately toss it with the tablespoon of softened butter. Add the chicken strips to the bowl, mixing them in lightly. Add the thick yogurt and toss quickly with the pasta and chicken to thoroughly mix them. Sprinkle with freshly grated black pepper and serve with a bowl of grated Parmesan cheese.

Accompany this with a tossed green salad and broiled tomato halves. If good tomatoes are in season, serve fresh sliced tomatoes topped with chopped basil or parsley, with a little olive oil dribbled over them and a few drops of white wine vinegar or lemon juice sprinkled on. Alternatives might be chopped boiled spinach or a watercress and endive salad.

Yield: 4 servings.

**See page 16.

Baked Chicken

One 2½ to 3-pound chicken, cut up, or
   2 very large or 3 medium breasts, split, or
   2 very large or 3 medium breasts, split,
   skinned and boned

1 cup yogurt
1 or 2 cloves garlic, crushed
2 cups bread crumbs
¾ cup grated Parmesan or Romano cheese, or
   a mixture of both
¼ cup chopped parsley (preferably flat-leaf)
½ teaspoon salt
1/8 teaspoon pepper
2 tablespoons butter

Wash the chicken pieces and dry them thoroughly with paper towels. Place chicken pieces in a bowl or on a wide plate and pour the yogurt over them, turning the pieces so that they are coated on all sides with the yogurt. Let them sit for about 30 minutes, turning occasionally.

Preheat the oven to 350°.

While the chicken is marinating, combine the garlic, bread crumbs, grated cheese, parsley, salt and pepper. Mix thoroughly and spread on a sheet of wax paper.

Remove the chicken pieces from the yogurt and roll each piece in the bread crumb mixture to coat thoroughly, patting the crumbs lightly so that they will adhere better.

Place the chicken pieces on a greased ovenproof platter, and dot them with the butter.

If chicken pieces have bones, bake for 1 hour without turning. If using boned skinned breasts, bake for only 30 minutes.

Serve with zucchini, either sliced and steamed or shredded and sauteed with minced shallots and butter. Fresh asparagus, broccoli or string beans would also go well with this. A romaine salad would be a nice accompaniment too.

Yield: 4 to 6 servings.

Chickenburgers

2 large chicken breasts, boned and
  skinned (about 1 pound)
1 tablespoon minced onion, or
  1½ tablespoons minced shallots
1 cup bread crumbs
¼ cup yogurt cheese**
2 tablespoons minced parsley (preferably
  flat-leaf)
Salt and pepper to taste
2 tablespoons butter
2 tablespoons oil

Have the chicken breasts ground or grind them yourself.

Mix the ground chicken with the onion or shallots, ¾ cup of the bread crumbs, the yogurt cheese, parsley, salt and pepper. Blend thoroughly. Form the mixture into 4 patties. Dredge the patties in the remaining bread crumbs, patting the crumbs to make them adhere. Refrigerate the patties until you are ready to cook.

In a large heavy skillet, heat the butter and oil. Brown the patties for about 3 minutes on each side over moderately high heat.

Serve with buttered green beans tossed with sliced water chestnuts, along with steamed new potatoes rolled in melted butter and coarse salt.

Yield: 4 servings.

**See page 16.

Chicken with Lemon Sauce

Two 2-pound broilers, cut up, or
  3 large or 4 small chicken breasts, split
4 tablespoons butter or oil, or a
  combination of both
Salt and pepper to taste
½ cup dry white wine
Grated rind of 1 lemon
1 teaspoon lemon juice
1 cup thick yogurt**
¼ cup grated Parmesan cheese

Wash the chicken pieces and thoroughly pat dry.

In a large heavy pan, heat the butter or oil, add the chicken pieces and brown them on all sides. When they are brown, salt and pepper them lightly, add the wine, lemon rind and juice, cover the pan tightly and cook the chicken over low heat for about 30 minutes.

If not serving immediately, set the covered pan aside. When ready, heat the chicken very briefly before proceeding to the next step.

Preheat the broiler.

Remove the chicken pieces from the pan and place them on a heatproof platter. Add the thick yogurt to the pan juices and heat, stirring, over moderate heat. Pour the hot sauce over the chicken, sprinkle the grated cheese on top and broil for about 5 minutes, until the top is golden brown.

Serve with broccoli or asparagus and steamed new potatoes rolled in parsley butter.

Yield: 4 servings.

**See page 16.

Curried Chicken Breasts

2 large or 3 small chicken breasts,
   skinned and boned
1 cup drained yogurt**
Salt to taste
2 teaspoons grated fresh ginger, or
   ½ teaspoon powdered ginger
1/8 teaspoon cayenne pepper
2 tablespoons clarified butter or oil
1 small onion, minced
½ tart apple, peeled, cored and finely chopped
1 stalk celery, finely chopped
1 tablespoon curry powder (or to taste)

Cube the chicken and place in a bowl.

Mix the drained yogurt with salt, ginger and cayenne and pour over the chicken, turning the cubes over and over in the yogurt so that they are thoroughly coated. Marinate the chicken in the yogurt for about 30 minutes.

In a large heavy skillet, heat the clarified butter or oil and sauté the onion, apple and celery over moderate heat until they are tender, stirring occasionally. Do not let them brown. Sprinkle with the curry powder and cook, stirring, for about 2 minutes.

Add the chicken and yogurt marinade to the pan. Mix well and heat until the mixture comes just to a boil. Immediately lower the heat. Cover the pan and simmer over very low heat for about 10 minutes, or until the chicken is tender.

Serve with boiled rice, a bowl of thick yogurt** and the classic accompaniments—bowls of chutney, peanuts, raisins, sliced bananas. Additional accompaniments might be thinly sliced cucumbers,which have been sprinkled with salt and allowed to stand for 30 minutes before being drained, and cooked lentils.

Yield: 4 servings.

**See page 16.

Chicken Loaf

2 cups diced cooked chicken (or turkey)
½ cup chopped celery
½ cup chopped carrots
¼ cup chopped onion
¾ cup bread crumbs
1 egg
1 tablespoon lemon juice
1 teaspoon fresh tarragon, or
   ½ teaspoon crushed dried tarragon
¼ teaspoon salt
¼ teaspoon pepper
½ cup yogurt cheese**
Grilled tomatoes or baked cherry tomatoes
Watercress

Preheat the oven to 350°.

Combine the chicken, celery, carrots, onion and bread crumbs in a bowl.

Beat together the egg, lemon juice, tarragon, salt, pepper and yogurt cheese, and add to the chicken mixture. Mix thoroughly to blend and turn into a greased 8½" x 4½" x 2-5/8" (or 6 cup) loaf pan.

Set the loaf pan in a larger pan containing enough hot water to come halfway up the side of the loaf pan. Bake for about 50 to 60 minutes.

To serve, invert pan on platter and garnish with grilled tomatoes or baked cherry tomatoes and watercress.

Serve with boiled rice and a bowl of Mushroom Sauce (see page 162).

Yield: 4 to 6 servings.

**See page 16.

Chicken with Mushrooms and Artichoke Hearts

4 tablespoons butter
2 tablespoons minced shallots, or
*   1 tablespoon minced onion*
¼ pound mushrooms, sliced
3 tablespoons flour
1 cup boiling chicken stock or broth
½ cup dry vermouth or dry white wine
*½ cup yogurt cream** or thick yogurt***
Salt and pepper to taste
¼ teaspoon crushed dried tarragon
About 3 cups cooked chicken in large pieces (see Note)
One or two 8½-ounce cans artichoke hearts, well
*   drained, or two 9-ounce packages frozen*
*   artichoke hearts, cooked*
3 or 4 tablespoons minced parsley
One 15-ounce can imported whole
*   baby carrots, or 1 pound cooked*
*   baby carrots (optional)*

In a large heavy pan, melt 2 tablespoons of the butter and sauté the shallots or onion until soft and translucent but not brown. Add the sliced mushrooms and sauté them gently for about 4 or 5 minutes. Remove the contents of the pan (including the juices) to a side dish.

In the same pan, melt the remaining 2 tablespoons of butter and blend in the flour. Cook over moderate heat for 2 or 3 minutes, stirring. Do not let it brown.

Remove the pan from the heat and add the boiling chicken stock all at once, stirring briskly with a wire whisk to incorporate the roux. Return the pan to the heat and cook the sauce for a minute or two, stirring, then add the vermouth or wine. Add the yogurt cream or thick yogurt gradually, stirring until the sauce is thick and smooth and starting to bubble. Blend in the salt, pepper and tarragon.

Lower the heat and add the chicken to the sauce. Add the shallots or onion, mushrooms and their juices. Add the artichoke hearts and carrots, and cook gently until all ingredients are heated through.

Serve with boiled rice tossed with melted butter and minced parsley, and a mixed green salad.

Yield: 4 to 6 servings.

Note: The cooked chicken called for in this recipe could be from poached chicken breasts. For 6 servings, figure on 2 very large, 3 large or 4 small breasts (1 pound with bones is a generous serving). You could also poach cut-up chicken or boil a whole stewing chicken (see directions under recipe for Baked Chicken and Wild Rice or Noodles, page 90).

**See page 16.

Chicken Livers with Mushrooms

1 pound chicken livers
¼ cup flour
½ teaspoon salt
¼ teaspoon pepper
6 tablespoons butter
2 tablespoons minced shallots, or
*   1½ tablespoons minced onion*
1 clove garlic, crushed
½ pound mushrooms, thinly sliced
¼ cup dry vermouth
½ teaspoon crushed dried sage
¼ teaspoon crushed dried thyme
*1 cup thick yogurt***

Clean the chicken livers and cut each one in half. Mix the flour with the salt and pepper and dredge the livers in this mixture.

In a large heavy skillet, heat 3 tablespoons of the butter over moderate heat and add the chicken livers. Cook the livers on all sides, turning them (wooden tongs or chopsticks are useful for this) until they are just browned. Set aside the livers, pouring the pan juices over them.

In the same skillet, melt the remaining 3 tablespoons butter and add the shallots or onion and the garlic. Cook for about a minute over moderate heat, then add the mushrooms. Cook, stirring, for about 3 or 4 minutes.

Return the livers to the pan and cook them briefly with the shallots or onion, the garlic and mushrooms. Add the vermouth, sage and thyme. Continue cooking over moderate heat for about 3 or 4 minutes, or until livers have almost reached the desired degree of doneness. Add the thick yogurt, stirring to blend thoroughly. Let all the ingredients cook together for another minute or so, but do not let the sauce boil.

Serve with rice or noodles, broiled tomatoes or chopped spinach and a salad of watercress and endive.

Yield: 4 servings.

**See page 16.

Baked Chicken with Wild Rice (or Noodles)

About 4 cups large chunks of cooked chicken
(see Note)
4 tablespoons butter or rendered chicken fat
3 tablespoons flour
2 cups boiling chicken stock
1/3 cup dry white wine or dry vermouth
*½ cup thick yogurt***
Salt and pepper to taste
¼ teaspoon nutmeg
1/8 teaspoon thyme

One 8-ounce package wild rice, or
    8 ounces noodles
½ pound mushrooms, sliced (optional)
2 tablespoons butter

In a large heavy saucepan, melt the 4 tablespoons of butter or fat and blend in the flour. Cook over moderate heat for about 2 minutes, stirring. Do not let the mixture brown.

Remove the pan from the heat and add the boiling chicken stock all at once, stirring briskly with a wire whisk to incorporate the roux. Return the pan to the heat and cook the sauce for a minute or two, stirring. Add the wine or vermouth gradually, stirring, and blend in the thick yogurt. Add the salt, pepper, nutmeg and thyme. Cook the sauce for a few minutes, until it is thick and smooth. Taste and adjust seasonings.

Remove pan from the heat and set aside. To prevent a skin from forming on the sauce, film it with a little melted butter or milk, or press a piece of clear plastic wrap gently onto the surface so that it is airtight.

If you are using wild rice, while the rice is cooking, sauté the mushrooms in 2 tablespoons melted butter until tender, and season to taste with salt and pepper. Set aside. Toss the cooked rice with the mushrooms and their juices. Taste and adjust seasonings.

If you are using noodles, cook according to package directions until they are barely tender (remember they will cook further in the oven). Drain them and rinse in warm water. Drain them again.

Preheat the oven to 375°.

In a large greased ovenproof serving dish with a cover, arrange half of the rice-and-mushroom mixture or half of the noodles. Spread the chicken over this layer. Top with the other half of the rice or noodles. Reheat the sauce until it just starts to bubble and pour it evenly over the top layer of rice or noodles. Cover the dish and bake until heated through, about 25 or 30 minutes.

Serve with spiced crabapples or spiced pears, and a mixed green salad of Boston lettuce, watercress and escarole. If you did not use mushrooms in the casserole, add a few sliced raw mushrooms to the salad and perhaps some very thin slices of raw zucchini.

Yield: 8 servings.

Note: The cooked chicken can come from the following:

• 2 broilers (about 3 pounds each), cut up, or 3 very large or 4 medium breasts. Either broil them (be careful not to overcook or let them get dry) or simmer them gently as follows: In a large saucepan, cover the chicken pieces with cold water, add a bay leaf, a few parsley stems, a garlic clove, a few peppercorns, salt, a celery stalk and a small onion studded with a clove. Bring the water just to the boil, lower the heat and simmer the chicken for 15 minutes. After 15 minutes, turn off the heat and let chicken cool in the stock. When cool enough to handle, remove chicken from stock and remove meat from bones, discarding bones and skin. Strain stock and reserve for other purposes.

• Stew a chicken as follows: Place a 5-pound stewing chicken in a large pot along with 2 celery stalks, a quartered carrot, a large onion studded with a clove, 6 parsley stems, a bay leaf, a few peppercorns and some salt. Pour in 4 to 5 cups boiling water. Bring to a boil again over moderate heat. Lower the heat, cover the pan and simmer gently about 3 hours, until chicken is tender. Let chicken cool in stock. When cool enough to handle, remove chicken from stock, and remove meat from bones, discarding bones and skin. Skim fat from stock, strain and reduce stock to 2 cups; reserve stock for other purposes.

**See page 16.

Tongue in Mushroom Sauce

3 tablespoons butter
½ pound mushrooms, sliced
3 tablespoons flour
Salt and pepper to taste
1/8 teaspoon nutmeg
1½ cups yogurt
1 teaspoon grated lemon rind
2 cups diced cooked tongue
2 tablespoons minced parsley

In a heavy pan, melt the butter and sauté the mushrooms for about 5 minutes, until tender. Remove the mushrooms with a slotted spoon to a side dish.

Add the flour to the pan and stir to blend thoroughly with the butter and mushroom juices. Cook together over moderate heat for a minute or two. Add the salt, pepper and nutmeg and slowly add the yogurt, stirring, until the sauce is thick and smooth. Add the lemon rind and return the mushrooms to the pan. Add the tongue and stir. Taste and adjust seasonings. When hot and bubbling, place on a serving dish and sprinkle with minced parsley.

Serve with baked or mashed potatoes, and boiled sliced beets or cold pickled beets.

Yield: 4 servings.

Note: This can be prepared ahead of time, placed in an ovenproof baking dish and refrigerated. Bake in a preheated 350° oven for about 25 minutes.

Tongue in Mustard Sauce

½ cup Madeira
Few drops tabasco
1½ pounds thinly sliced cooked tongue
¾ cup reduced tongue stock, or
* ¾ cup strong beef bouillon*
½ cup thick yogurt**
1 tablespoon Dijon or Burgundy mustard
Salt, if necessary
Minced parsley

In a large pan, stir the stock, Madeira and tabasco over moderate heat. Add the tongue slices and let them heat in the broth, turning them frequently so they absorb the juices, until they are piping hot. Remove the tongue slices to a platter, lower the heat, add the thick yogurt and mustard to the pan and cook, stirring, until the sauce is smooth and just hot. Taste and add salt if necessary. Pour the sauce over the tongue slices and sprinkle with minced parsley.

Accompany the tongue with small sour pickles and spinach, which is the classic accompaniment to tongue. Mashed turnips or a puree of potatoes and turnips would also go well.

Yield: 6 servings.

**See page 16.

Ham and Noodle Casserole

1 pound noodles or linguine (preferably green)
4 tablespoons butter
½ pound mushrooms, sliced
3 tablespoons flour
2 cups yogurt
½ cup sweet cream or
evaporated skim milk (undiluted)
Salt and pepper to taste
¼ teaspoon nutmeg
Pinch of ground cloves
1 cup grated Swiss or Gruyère cheese
mixed with 1 cup grated Parmesan cheese
12 pitted black olives, quartered (about ½ cup)
4 cups diced cooked ham (preferably baked)

Preheat the oven to 375°.

While salted water for the noodles or linguine is coming to a boil, make the sauce.

In a large heavy skillet, melt 3 tablespoons of the butter and sauté the mushrooms until they are tender. Push the mushrooms to one side of the pan and add the flour, blending it thoroughly. Cook over low heat for a few minutes. Add the yogurt and sweet cream or evaporated skim milk, stirring to make a smooth sauce, and add seasonings. Beat in 1½ cups of the grated cheese and let the sauce come to a gentle boil. Add the olives and ham.

Cook the pasta in boiling salted water until almost done (remember, it will cook further in the oven). Drain pasta and rinse in warm water.

Butter 2½- or 3-quart casserole with ½ tablespoon of the remaining butter. Spread a third of the noodles in the bottom of the casserole and top with a third of the sauce. Make another layer of half the remaining noodles and half the remaining sauce, and repeat with the rest of the noodles and sauce.

Just before placing in the oven, sprinkle with the remaining ½ cup of grated cheese and dot the top with the remaining ½ table-spoon of butter, cut into small bits. Bake until top is lightly browned and bubbling, about 30 to 40 minutes.

Serve with sliced tomatoes or cold boiled string beans vinaigrette.

Yield: 8 to 10 servings.

Note: This can be prepared in advance, but defer topping it with cheese and butter until just before placing it in the oven.

VARIATIONS

Substitute cooked chicken or turkey, or tuna fish which has been thoroughly drained (and rinsed if packed in oil) for the ham.

Moussaka

2 medium eggplants (about 2 pounds)
1 teaspoon salt
¼ cup olive or vegetable oil
1 medium onion, chopped
1 pound ground lean lamb or beef
2 cups Basic Tomato Sauce (see page 166)
¼ cup minced parsley (preferably flat-leaf)
2 cloves garlic, minced
¼ teaspoon cinnamon
Salt and pepper to taste
½ cup bread crumbs
½ cup grated Parmesan cheese
2 eggs, beaten
1 cup yogurt

Preheat the oven to 350°.

Peel the eggplants and cut them lengthwise into slices about ¼ to ½ inch thick. Sprinkle the slices with a teaspoon of salt and allow them to drain in a colander or on paper towels for about 30 minutes while you make the meat sauce.

In a large heavy skillet, heat the oil over moderate heat. Add the chopped onion to the skillet and cook, stirring occasionally, until soft and translucent but not brown. Add the meat and cook, stirring and breaking it up until it loses its red color. Add the tomato sauce, parsley, garlic, cinnamon, salt and pepper, and cook over moderate heat about 15 to 20 minutes, until the sauce is very thick. Taste and adjust seasonings. Remove pan from heat.

Rinse the eggplant slices in cold water to remove the salt, and dry thoroughly with paper towels.

Lightly oil a rectangular ovenproof pan or baking dish (about 9" x 12" x 2"). Cover the bottom of the pan with half the eggplant slices, cutting them to fit so that they make a solid layer of eggplant. Spread the eggplant with half of the meat sauce, cover with the remaining eggplant and the rest of the sauce.

Sprinkle with half of the bread crumbs and half of the grated cheese.

Add the beaten eggs to the yogurt, blending thoroughly with a fork.

Pour the egg-and-yogurt mixture evenly over the top of the bread crumb and cheese layer, spreading it quickly to cover the entire surface; sprinkle with the remaining bread crumbs and cheese.

Bake until the top is light brown and crusty and the eggplant seems tender (but not soft and mushy) when tested with a fork, about 1 hour. If the top browns too soon, cover it loosely with aluminum foil until done.

Let cool slightly before serving (it tastes better warm than hot—it is also good cold). Cut into rectangular pieces to serve.

Serve with rice and a large mixed green salad, followed by Baked Lemon Pudding (see page 197).

Yield: 6 servings.

Note: If you are assembling the casserole in advance, wait until you are ready to place it in the preheated oven before pouring on the egg-and-yogurt mixture and sprinkling on the topping.

Macaroni and Beef Casserole

¼ cup olive or vegetable oil
1 medium onion, chopped
2 pounds ground lean beef (or lamb)
2 cups Basic Tomato Sauce (see page 166)
¼ cup dry white wine
¼ cup chopped parsley (preferably flat-leaf)
1 clove garlic, crushed
Salt and pepper to taste
Pinch of nutmeg
1 pound elbow macaroni or spaghetti
4 tablespoons very soft butter
3 eggs, beaten with ¼ teaspoon salt
1 tablespoon butter
3 tablespoons grated Parmesan cheese
3 cups Basic White (Béchamel) Sauce
   (see page 159)

In a large heavy skillet, heat the oil over moderate heat. Add the chopped onion and cook, stirring occasionally, until the onion is soft and translucent, but not brown. Add the meat and cook, stirring and breaking up the meat, until it loses its red color. Add the tomato sauce, wine, parsley, garlic, salt, pepper and nutmeg, and cook over moderate heat about 15 to 20 minutes, until the sauce is very thick. Taste and adjust seasonings. Remove pan from heat.

Preheat the oven to 350°.

Cook the pasta according to package directions until it is slightly underdone with a definite chewy texture. Drain the cooked pasta in a colander, rinse it with warm water and turn it into a large warmed bowl. Add the soft butter and the beaten eggs and toss the pasta gently but thoroughly to coat it.

Butter a large shallow baking dish (about 9" x 14" x 2") with the tablespoon of butter. Spread half of the cooked pasta evenly on the bottom of the pan and sprinkle it with 1 tablespoon of the grated cheese. Top this layer with half of the meat sauce. Repeat with the rest of the pasta, 1 tablespoon of cheese and the balance of the meat sauce, spread evenly and smoothly on the top. Cover the entire surface with the white sauce, spreading it evenly. Sprinkle with the last tablespoon of the cheese and bake until the top is golden brown, about 50 minutes.

Serve with a raw mushroom and spinach salad or a mixed green vegetable.

Yield: 8 to 10 servings.

Note: Both sauces can be prepared a day in advance and refrigerated. Be sure to film the surface of the white sauce with about 2 teaspoons melted butter or milk, or cover the surface with a piece of clear plastic wrap, pressing it down lightly to make an airtight seal. Either method prevents a skin from forming on the sauce. Reheat the sauces over low heat while cooking the pasta.

Stuffed Green Peppers

4 large green peppers (choose firm ones with
*   shiny, unwrinkled skins)*
2 tablespoons butter
2 tablespoons minced shallots, or
*   1½ tablespoons minced onion*
¼ pound mushrooms, chopped
1½ cups diced cooked ham
3/4 cup cooked rice
¼ cup thick yogurt**
Salt and pepper to taste
1 tablespoon minced parsley
Basic Tomato Sauce (optional—see page 166)

Preheat the oven to 350°.

Wash the peppers, slice off their tops and remove the seeds and membranes from their insides. Place the peppers in a colander or sieve and put them into a pot containing boiling water to cover. Let them boil for about 3 or 4 minutes, then remove and drain them. Or, place them in a vegetable steamer over a small quantity of boiling water and steam them for about 3 or 4 minutes; remove and drain.

In a heavy pan, melt the butter and sauté the shallots or onion over low heat until soft and tender. Add the mushrooms to the pan and sauté them until tender, about 5 minutes. Add the ham, rice and thick yogurt, mixing thoroughly. Add the salt and pepper. Taste and adjust the seasonings. When the filling is hot, remove it from the heat and fill the pepper shells with the mixture.

Place the filled peppers in a buttered ovenproof dish that will accommodate them snugly, and pour ¼ cup of water around the peppers. Bake them until peppers are tender, about 15 minutes. Sprinkle them with minced parsley before serving with tomato sauce.

VARIATIONS

Use cooked chicken, veal or pork in place of the ham. Substitute celery and tuna fish for the mushrooms and ham. Brown ½ pound of ground beef or lamb with the onions and mushrooms. Increase the meat in the filling and serve the rice separately.

**See page 16.

Persian Eggplant

1 large or 2 medium eggplants (about 1½ pounds)
2 tablespoons butter or oil
½ cup minced onion
1 pound ground beef or lamb
*½ cup yogurt cheese***
¼ cup minced parsley
¼ teaspoon dried basil
¼ teaspoon coriander
Salt and pepper to taste
3 tablespoons bread crumbs

3 tablespoons Parmesan or Gruyère cheese
3 tablespoons melted butter

Wash the eggplants and cut off their green caps. Cook the eggplants by steaming them in a vegetable rack or sieve set over (but not touching) boiling water in a tightly covered pan for about 15 to 20 minutes, depending on size. Or, bake the eggplants in a preheated 425° oven for about 25 to 35 minutes. Before baking, pierce the skin on each side in 2 or 3 places with the point of a knife and place them in an oiled baking pan.

When the eggplants are cooked (they should be soft all over, but not mushy), cut them in half lengthwise and scoop out the flesh, making sure not to break the skin. Place the eggplant pulp in a bowl and reserve the shells for filling.

Preheat the oven to 350°.

Melt the butter or oil in a heavy pan over moderate heat, add the minced onion and cook it until it is limp and tender. Add the meat and cook, stirring and breaking it up, until it loses its red color. Add the meat and the onion to the bowl containing the eggplant pulp.

In a separate bowl, mash and soften the yogurt cheese with a fork. Add the parsley, basil and coriander. Mix thoroughly and add this mixture to the meat-and-eggplant mixture. Add salt and pepper to taste and mix all together thoroughly.

Fill the eggplant shells with the mixture. Mix the bread crumbs with the grated cheese and sprinkle this over the stuffed shells. Place the eggplant halves in a roasting pan and dribble melted butter over the tops. Pour a small amount of hot water (about ¼ inch) around the eggplants in the pan and bake in the upper third of the oven until the tops are lightly browned, about 25 to 30 minutes. Serve an eggplant half to each guest if you used 2 medium ones, or divide in quarters if the eggplant was large.

Yield: 4 servings.

Note: This dish can be prepared in advance. In that case, the bread crumb-and-cheese topping and melted butter should not be added until just before baking.

**See page 16.

Vegetables

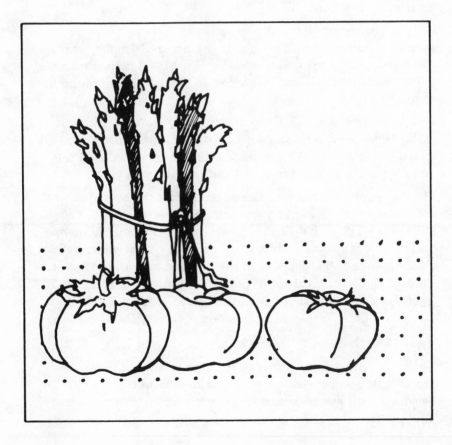

Quick and Easy Vegetables

BEETS

Slice or shred cooked beets. Mix thick yogurt** with minced onion or horseradish and toss with the beets. Serve hot or cold.

CUCUMBERS

Peel cucumbers, split them lengthwise and scoop out the seeds. Cut the halves into halves or thirds. Cook in boiling salted water for about 5 minutes. Toss with thick yogurt** and minced fresh dill or dried dill.

EGGPLANT

Peel eggplant and cut into ½-inch cubes. Cook the cubes in about ½ inch boiling salted water. Drain well and set aside. Melt a tablespoon of butter in the pan, add a tablespoon of grated onion and cook briefly. Add thick yogurt** and the eggplant cubes. Toss well, and add salt and pepper to taste. Cook until heated through. Sprinkle with minced parsley.

PEAS

Combine frozen peas, cooked and drained, with cucumber, peeled, seeded, diced and cooked in boiling salted water for 2 minutes. Toss vegetables while hot with thick yogurt** and minced fresh dill.

POTATOES

Baked—Just before serving, split the potato and top with minced fresh dill added to thick yogurt**, or minced chives or scallion stems mixed with thick yogurt**.

Boiled—Slice thickly and toss with a mixture of dill or chives and thick yogurt**.

RADISHES

Trim stem and root ends from radishes. Boil in salted water for about 15 minutes. Drain them and toss with yogurt and minced parsley.

**See page 16.

RICE

Mix thick yogurt** and minced parsley or chives with hot cooked rice. Or, sauté sliced fresh mushrooms with a little butter, salt and pepper for about 5 minutes. Blend thick yogurt** into the pan juices and toss with hot rice.

TOMATOES

Cut large ones in half horizontally, or just cut off the tops of small ones. Sprinkle tops with a little salt. Spread the tops with a mixture of half mayonnaise and half yogurt cheese** mixed with minced parsley, chives or dill. Broil for about 5 minutes, until tops are golden and slightly puffy. Or, mix the mayonnaise with yogurt cheese** and add curry powder to taste.

**See page 16.

Baked Asparagus

1 pound asparagus
4 eggs
1 tablespoon lemon juice
Salt and pepper to taste
*1 cup drained yogurt***
Pinch of cayenne pepper (optional)

Preheat the oven to 350°.

Snap off and discard the tough ends of the asparagus. Wash the stalks well and cut them into thin diagonal slices. Cook in boiling salted water (just enough to cover them) for about 5 minutes. Drain the asparagus thoroughly.

While the asparagus is cooking, beat the eggs with the lemon juice. Add the salt and pepper and gently stir in the drained yogurt. Mix well, adding the cayenne.

Pour about a third of the egg-and-yogurt sauce into a lightly buttered baking dish. Place the asparagus pieces on the sauce base. Cover them with the rest of the sauce.

Place the baking dish in a pan of hot water in the lower third of the oven. Bake for about 30 minutes.

Yield: 4 servings.

**See page 16.

Creamed Green Beans

2 pounds fresh green beans, or
   two 10-ounce packages frozen green beans
2 tablespoons butter
1 tablespoon minced shallots or onion
1 to 2 teaspoons wine vinegar
2 tablespoons flour
*¾ cup thick yogurt***
Salt and pepper to taste
Few sliced water chestnuts or
   sliced sautéed mushrooms (optional)
1 tablespoon minced parsley

If you are using fresh green beans, wash and trim them. Cook fresh or frozen beans until they are just tender.

In a skillet, melt the butter and add the shallots or onion. Cook over low heat for a few minutes until they are soft but not brown. Add the vinegar and cook for just a minute, then blend in the flour. Cook the butter and flour together for about 2 or 3 minutes, then add the thick yogurt, salt and pepper. Let the sauce come to a boil over moderate heat, stirring occasionally, until the sauce is smooth. Fold in the beans and water chestnuts or mushrooms, and garnish with minced parsley.

Yield: 4 to 6 servings.

**See page 16.

Creamed Brussels Sprouts

*2 pints fresh Brussels sprouts (about 1¼ pounds), or
    two 10-ounce packages frozen Brussels sprouts*
3 tablespoons butter
3 tablespoons flour
2 cups yogurt
½ teaspoon salt (or to taste)
1/8 teaspoon marjoram
Pinch of nutmeg
Pepper to taste
¼ cup grated Swiss or mild Cheddar cheese
Small bits of butter

Cook the Brussels sprouts until they are just tender. Drain them and spread them out on a paper towel in 1 layer.

Preheat the broiler.

In a heavy pan, melt the butter and add the flour, stirring to blend well. Let them cook together for about 2 or 3 minutes, then add the yogurt. Cook over moderate heat, stirring, until sauce is bubbly and smooth. Add seasonings and cook for a minute. Taste and adjust seasonings.

Lightly butter a low baking dish (a round one about 9 inches in diameter and 2 inches deep would be fine). Cover the bottom of the dish with about a third of the sauce. Arrange the cooked Brussels sprouts on the sauce base. Pour the rest of the sauce over the sprouts. Top with grated cheese and dot with bits of butter. Place under the broiler until top is lightly browned, about 4 or 5 minutes.

Yield: 4 to 6 servings.

Carrot and Potato Puree

4 medium potatoes (about 1 pound)
4 to 6 carrots (about ¾ pound)
1 egg, lightly beaten
¼ cup thick yogurt**
Salt and pepper to taste
½ teaspoon Dijon-type mustard
3 tablespoons grated mild cheese
1 tablespoon butter

Scrub and peel the potatoes and cut in slices. Wash and scrape the carrots and cut into long slices. Place the potatoes and carrots in a pan with enough boiling salted water to cover, and cook them until they are soft. Preheat the broiler.

Drain and mash the vegetables. Put the mixture through a food mill or puree in a blender. Mix well with the beaten egg, thick yogurt, salt, pepper and mustard. Place in a shallow buttered baking dish, and sprinkle with grated cheese. Dot with bits of butter and brown under a broiler.

Yield: 4 servings.

**See page 16.

Spiced Carrots

4 to 6 carrots (about ¾ pound)
¼ teaspoon salt
½ teaspoon sugar
2 tablespoons butter
1 tablespoon minced shallots
   or scallions
2 tablespoons flour
¼ teaspoon dry mustard
¼ teaspoon powdered ginger
1/8 teaspoon pepper
½ cup yogurt
Minced parsley

Scrape and slice or dice the carrots (there should be about 4 cups) and place in a pan. Add boiling water to just cover them, and add the salt and sugar. Cover the pan and cook for about 7 or 8 minutes, until carrots are tender. Drain the carrots, reserving ½ cup of the cooking water.

In the same pan, melt the butter over low heat and cook the minced shallots or scallions for a few minutes until they are soft and limp but not brown. Add the flour and stir to blend. Add the mustard, ginger and pepper, then the carrot cooking water. Stir to blend thoroughly and add the yogurt. Stir until sauce is thick and bubbly. Taste and adjust seasonings.

Add the carrots to the sauce, and stir to blend. Serve sprinkled with a little minced parsley.

Yield: 4 servings.

Baked Cauliflower

1 medium head cauliflower (about 1½ pounds)
3 tablespoons melted butter
3 eggs, separated
½ teaspoon salt
Pepper to taste
¼ teaspoon nutmeg
1 cup thick yogurt**
3 tablespoons bread crumbs
½ cup grated mild cheese
   (Gruyère, mild Cheddar, etc.)
¼ teaspoon paprika

Trim the cauliflower, removing the leaves and most of the stem (save these for soups or Green Vegetable Dip—see page 20). Break the head up into florets and place them in a bowl of cold water for 20 minutes.

Preheat the oven to 375°.

Cook the florets in a large quantity of boiling salted water until barely tender, about 10 to 12 minutes. Drain and set aside.

Mix together the melted butter, egg yolks, salt, pepper, nutmeg, thick yogurt and bread crumbs. Beat the egg whites with a pinch of salt until they form soft peaks. Fold the whites into yolk-and-yogurt mixture.

Lightly butter a shallow baking dish and spread a third of the egg-and-yogurt mixture on the bottom. Arrange the florets in the dish and pour the rest of the mixture over them. Sprinkle the grated cheese and paprika on top and bake in the lower third of the oven for about 25 minutes until golden brown.

Yield: 4 servings.

Note: Broccoli can be substituted for the cauliflower.

**See page 16.

Curried Celery

2 cups sliced celery
2 tablespoons butter or oil
1 small onion, sliced
1 medium-size green cooking apple
1 teaspoon lemon juice
2 teaspoons curry powder (or to taste)
1 tablespoon flour
1/3 cup yogurt
½ teaspoon salt
1/8 teaspoon pepper (or to taste)

Cook the sliced celery in a small amount of boiling salted water (just enough to cover) for about 5 minutes. The celery should still be crisp. Drain.

In a heavy pan, melt the butter or oil over moderate heat and cook the onion for 2 minutes or so, until it is soft and translucent but not brown.

Peel, core and dice the apple and toss it with the lemon juice to prevent discoloration. Add the diced apple to the onion, then add the curry powder, stirring to blend it in with the butter, onion and apple. Cook for 1 or 2 minutes. Sprinkle with the flour and add the yogurt, salt and pepper. Stir and cook until the mixture is hot and bubbling slightly. Add the celery to the sauce. Stir gently to mix everything together.

Yield: 4 servings.

Hot Coleslaw

1 medium cabbage (about 1½ pounds)
½ cup thick yogurt**
1/3 cup mayonnaise
2 tablespoons wine vinegar
1 teaspoon Dijon-type mustard

1 teaspoon salt
1 teaspoon sugar
½ teaspoon caraway seeds or dill seeds
Pepper to taste

Quarter the cabbage and remove the tough core (this is good chopped and added to soups, or sliced and used as a raw vegetable with dip). Shred the cabbage (there should be about 4 cups).

In a serving bowl, mix together all the other ingredients.

In a large saucepan, bring 3 quarts of salted water to a boil. Place the shredded cabbage in the boiling water and cook it for 2 or 3 minutes. Drain the cabbage thoroughly in a large colander (or a smaller strainer set in the colander) using the back of a large spoon to press out all the liquid.

Add the hot cabbage to the serving bowl containing the sauce, toss well to blend and serve immediately.

Yield: 6 servings.

**See page 16.

Corn Pudding

1 tablespoon butter or oil
1 tablespoon minced onion
2 eggs
*¾ cup yogurt cheese***
One 16-ounce can cream-style corn
¼ teaspoon Worcestershire
¼ teaspoon salt
1/8 teaspoon pepper
4 thin slices Canadian bacon (about 2 ounces)

Preheat the oven to 350°.

In a small pan, melt the butter or oil and cook the minced onion over low heat for a few minutes until it is limp but not brown. Remove from heat.

Beat the eggs lightly and add to them the onion and yogurt cheese. Mix well, then add the corn and the seasonings.
Butter a shallow 4-cup baking dish (such as a small soufflé dish). Pour in the corn mixture and top with the Canadian bacon.

Bake in the lower third of the oven until the bacon is crisp at the edges, about 30 to 40 minutes.

Yield: 4 servings.

**See page 16. .

Baked Stuffed Eggplant

1 large or 2 small eggplants (about 1½ pounds)
¾ cup minced onion
1 tablespoon butter or oil
Salt and pepper to taste
½ pound mushrooms for
      1 cup of Duxelles (see page 161), or
      1 cup cooked rice or a combination of both
*½ cup yogurt cheese**
2 tablespoons minced parsley (preferably flat-leaf)
Pinch of thyme
2 tablespoons bread crumbs mixed with
      2 tablespoons grated Gruyère or Swiss cheese
1 tablespoon melted butter

Wash the eggplant and cut off the green top. Cook whole by either of the following methods:

Steaming: Place in a steamer, colander or sieve, and set over boiling water in a tightly covered pan. Do not let the water touch the eggplant. Steam for about 15 minutes. Test for doneness with a cake tester or skewer—it should be soft but not mushy.

Baking: Preheat the oven to 425°. Pierce the eggplant in 2 or 3 places with a skewer or tip of a sharp knife, and put it in an oiled baking pan. Bake until soft but not mushy, about 25 minutes. You can serve the eggplant either in the skin or in a shallow baking dish.

When the eggplant is cool enough to handle, scoop the flesh out of the shell. If you are serving in the skin, leave about ¼ inch of flesh in the shell; otherwise remove all the flesh. Place the eggplant flesh in a bowl and mash it up with a fork.

In a heavy skillet, melt the butter or oil and cook the minced onion over low heat for about 10 minutes, until very soft, but not brown. Season with salt and pepper, and mix with the mashed eggplant.

Add the Duxelles, rice or combination of both to the eggplant.

Mash the yogurt cheese until it is slightly softened and mix in the parsley. Add this to the eggplant and blend thoroughly. Mix in the thyme. Taste and adjust seasonings.

If serving in the skin, fill the shell with the mixture, top with bread crumbs and cheese, and dribble a little melted butter on the top. Place in a shallow baking pan and pour in about ¼ inch of hot water. Place in the upper third of the oven and bake until the top is lightly browned, about 25 to 30 minutes.

If serving in a baking dish, pile the mixture into a lightly greased shallow dish, top with bread crumbs and cheese, and dribble a little melted butter on top. Bake in the upper third of the oven until lightly browned, about 25 minutes.

Yield: 4 servings.

**See page 16.

Baked Eggplant Slices

1 large or 2 medium eggplants (about 1½ pounds)
¾ cup yogurt cheese**
¼ cup bread crumbs
¼ cup grated Parmesan or Swiss cheese
Pinch of cayenne pepper (optional)
2 tablespoons melted butter or oil
Salt and pepper (optional)

Wash the eggplant, and cut off the top and a slice from the bottom. Do not peel. Cut crosswise into slices about 3/8 inch thick. If the eggplant is very fat, cut in half lengthwise before slicing.

Sprinkle the slices on both sides with salt and let them drain on paper towels for about 30 minutes. Pat them dry.

Preheat the oven to 375°.

Place the slices on an oiled cookie sheet. Spread the top of each slice with a layer of the yogurt cheese. Mix the bread crumbs with the grated cheese and the cayenne, and sprinkle on top of the eggplant slices. Dribble the melted butter or oil over the top of the slices. If you have used a mild cheese and/or omitted the cayenne, sprinkle a little salt and pepper on the slices.

Bake in the lower third of the oven until lightly browned, for about 20 minutes.

Yield: 4 to 6 servings.

**See page 16.

Curried Kidney Beans

Two 20-ounce cans kidney beans
2 tablespoons oil
1 small onion, minced
1 clove garlic, crushed
1 tablespoon curry powder (or to taste)

¼ teaspoon powdered ginger
¾ cup thick yogurt**
½ teaspoon salt (or to taste)

Empty the cans of beans into a large pot and heat them over moderate heat.

While the beans are heating, heat the oil in a large pan, add the onion and garlic and cook over moderate heat for several minutes, until soft but not brown. Add the curry powder and ginger, and let this mixture cook for several minutes. Stir to prevent sticking or scorching. Add the thick yogurt and stir to blend. Remove the pan from the heat.

When the beans have heated sufficiently, drain them and reserve their liquid. Fold the beans into the onion-and-yogurt mixture, mixing well. Add some of the bean liquid to the pan until the desired consistency is reached. (This will depend on what you are serving with the beans—rice would call for a thinner sauce.)

Yield: 4 to 6 servings.

**See page 16.

Baked Lima Beans

Two 10-ounce packages frozen lima beans,
*   cooked and drained*
¼ cup brown sugar
1½ teaspoons dry mustard
Salt and pepper to taste
1 cup thick yogurt **
1 teaspoon cornstarch
2 teaspoons water
4 slices Canadian bacon (about 2 ounces)

Preheat the oven to 350°.

Place the lima beans in a buttered shallow baking dish.

Mix the sugar with the mustard, salt and pepper.

Mix the thick yogurt with a paste made of the cornstarch and water, and add this to the sugar-and-mustard mixture. Beat the mixture to blend it thoroughly. Taste and adjust seasonings.

Pour the sauce over the lima beans, mixing gently. Top with the Canadian bacon and bake in the lower third of the oven for about 30 minutes until bacon is crisp.

Yield: 4 servings.

**See page 16.

Mushrooms au Gratin

3 tablespoons butter
1 pound mushrooms, sliced
2 tablespoons flour
*1 cup thick yogurt***
½ teaspoon lemon juice
Salt to taste
1/8 teaspoon nutmeg
Pinch of cayenne or black pepper
¼ cup grated Parmesan or Swiss cheese

Preheat the oven to 375°.

In a large skillet, melt the butter. Add the sliced mushrooms and sauté over low heat for about 5 minutes or until they are soft. Using a slotted spoon, remove the mushrooms to a shallow baking dish, leaving the juices in the pan. Add the flour to the pan juices, stirring to blend, and let it cook for about 3 minutes. Add the thick yogurt and stir until sauce is bubbling and smooth. Add the lemon juice, salt, nutmeg and cayenne or black pepper. Taste and adjust seasonings.

Pour the hot sauce over the mushrooms in the baking dish, stirring to mix well. Sprinkle with grated cheese and bake until top is brown, about 25 minutes.

Yield: 4 to 6 servings.

**See page 16.

Baked Stuffed Mushrooms

12 large or 18 medium mushrooms
2 tablespoons melted butter
2 tablespoons minced shallots or scallions
2 tablespoons butter
1 tablespoon oil
Salt and pepper
2 to 3 tablespoons bread crumbs
3 tablespoons minced cooked ham or chicken
2 tablespoons minced parsley
¼ cup yogurt cheese**
3 tablespoons grated Swiss or Gruyère cheese
2 tablespoons melted butter

Wipe the mushrooms with a damp paper towel and remove the stems. Brush the mushroom caps with 2 tablespoons melted butter and place them, hollow side up, in a lightly buttered shallow baking dish or roasting pan. Chop the stems and set them aside.

Preheat the oven to 375°.

Sauté the minced shallots or scallions in 2 tablespoons butter and the oil for about 2 or 3 minutes, until they are soft but not brown. Sprinkle with a little salt and pepper and add the chopped mushroom stems. Cook over moderate heat for about 4 or 5 minutes. Remove from heat. Mix in the bread crumbs. Add the ham or chicken, parsley and yogurt cheese, and mix well. The mixture should be firm enough to hold its shape in a spoon. If it is not firm enough, add more bread crumbs or yogurt cheese.

Fill the caps with the stuffing mixture and sprinkle the tops with the grated cheese. Dribble on 2 tablespoons melted butter.

Bake in the upper third of the oven until the tops are lightly browned, about 15 minutes.

Yield: 6 servings.

**See page 16.

Baked Mushrooms and Tomatoes

1 pound mushrooms
2 tablespoons butter
1 tablespoon oil
1½ cups chopped fresh tomatoes, peeled,
*   seeded and juiced, or 1½ cups canned*
*   tomatoes, well drained*
1 teaspoon lemon juice
½ teaspoon sugar
½ teaspoon salt (or to taste)
Pepper to taste
½ cup thick yogurt**

Preheat the oven to 350°.

Wipe the mushrooms with a damp paper towel, quarter them and sauté them in the butter and oil for about 5 minutes. Add the tomatoes and cook over moderate heat for about 3 or 4 minutes. Mix in the lemon juice, sugar, salt and pepper, and place mixture in a small, deep casserole. Bake for about 15 minutes until lightly bubbling.

Just before serving, spread the top with cold thick yogurt.

Yield: 4 to 6 servings.

**See page 16.

Peppers Stuffed with Rice and Walnuts

4 large green peppers
2 tablespoons butter or oil, or a
*   combination of both*
1 to 2 teaspoons minced onion
½ cup chopped mushrooms
2 cups cooked rice
½ cup chopped carrots

Salt and pepper to taste
1/3 cup chopped parsley or watercress
1/3 cup chopped walnuts (or other nuts)
½ cup yogurt cheese**
1 tablespoon grated Swiss, Parmesan or
mild cheddar cheese (optional)

Wash the peppers, slice off a small part of the tops and carefully scrape out the seeds and membranes.

Invert the peppers in a sieve or steamer, place in a tightly covered pot over boiling water and steam them for about 5 minutes. Remove them from the pan and invert them on paper towels to drain.

Preheat the oven to 350°.

In a large heavy pan or skillet, melt the butter or oil and cook the onion briefly until soft but not brown. Add the mushrooms and cook them over moderate heat for about 4 or 5 minutes. Add the rice and let it warm up. Add the carrots, salt and pepper. Remove the pan from the heat. Add the parsley or watercress and the chopped nuts, mixing lightly. Soften the yogurt cheese with a fork and blend it thoroughly with the rice mixture.

Spoon the rice mixture into the peppers (be careful not to pierce the skin), packing lightly. Sprinkle the cheese on top. Place the peppers in a baking dish that will accommodate them snugly and pour hot water into the dish to a depth of about ½ inch. Bake the peppers in the middle or upper third of the oven for about 20 minutes.

Yield: 4 servings.

Note: This recipe will yield about 5 cups of filling, or about 1¼ cups for each pepper. If you are not sure of the size of the peppers, fill them with water before you steam them to determine how much filling they will hold. You can then adjust the filling as necessary. If you like, substitute tomato juice or beef broth for the water in which the peppers bake.

**See page 16.

Curried Potatoes

6 medium potatoes (1½ to 2 pounds)
1 large or 2 small tomatoes
2 tablespoons butter or oil, or a
  combination of both
2 teaspoons curry powder (or to taste)
½ teaspoon salt
½ cup thick yogurt**
Pinch of cayenne pepper (optional)

Scrub and peel the potatoes and cook them in boiling salted water until they are tender. Remove potatoes from the boiling boiling water.

Drop the tomatoes in the same water for exactly 10 seconds to loosen the skin for easy peeling. Cut out the stem end of the tomatoes and peel them from the stem end down. Cut them in half horizontally, and squeeze them to pop out the seeds and the watery part of their juices. Chop the tomatoes coarsely and set them aside.

Slice the potatoes thickly (about ¼ or 3/8 inch) and set aside.

In a heavy pan or skillet, heat the butter or oil and add the curry powder and salt. Stir over moderate heat for a minute or so. Add 2 tablespoons of the thick yogurt and blend it with the curry. Add the sliced potatoes and turn them lightly until they are coated. Add the rest of the yogurt and cook for a minute or so over low heat. Add the chopped tomatoes and cayenne. Stir gently. Taste and adjust seasonings. Turn off heat. Cover the pan until ready to serve.

Yield: 4 to 6 servings.

**See page 16.

Potatoes and Celery Root au Gratin

2 large or 3 medium potatoes (about ¾ pound)
1 medium yellow onion
1 medium celery root (about ½ pound)
1 clove garlic
2 to 3 tablespoons butter
Salt and pepper to taste
1 cup drained yogurt**
½ teaspoon Dijon-type mustard.
1 egg, lightly beaten
2 tablespoons coarsely grated mild cheese
(Gruyère, mild Cheddar, etc.)
1 tablespoon bread crumbs

Preheat the oven to 400°.

Peel and thinly slice the potatoes and place them in cold water to prevent discoloration. Peel and slice thinly the onion and celery root.

Cut the garlic clove in half and rub the cut side on the inside of a shallow baking dish. Discard the garlic. Smear about 1 tablespoon of the butter on the bottom and sides of the baking dish.

Drain the potato slices and pat them dry with paper towels. Arrange a third of the potatoes in a layer on the bottom of the dish, sprinkle them with salt and pepper and dot them with bits of butter (about 1 teaspoon). Add a layer of half the onion slices and then a layer of half the celery root slices. Sprinkle with salt and pepper and dot with butter. Repeat the layers, using half of the potato slices and the balance of the onion and celery root slices, sprinkling with salt and pepper and dotting with little bits of butter. Top with the remaining potato slices.

Mix the drained yogurt and mustard and then add the beaten egg, blending well. Pour the mixture over the top of the baking dish and shake the dish gently to distribute the yogurt-and-mustard mixture evenly throughout the dish.

Sprinkle the top with the grated cheese and bread crumbs and dot with bits of butter.

Bake in the upper third of the oven for about 45 minutes until nicely browned. Check after 30 minutes, and if the top is browning too rapidly cover it loosely with some foil.

Yield: 4 servings.

**See page 16.

Potato and Cheese Pudding

2 cups hot mashed potatoes
*1 cup thick yogurt ***
1 cup cottage cheese
1 tablespoon grated onion
½ teaspoon salt (or to taste)
Pepper to taste
Pinch of nutmeg
2 eggs, well beaten
3 or 4 tablespoons grated Parmesan or
   sharp Cheddar cheese
1 tablespoon bread crumbs (optional)
1 to 2 tablespoons butter

Preheat the oven to 350°.

Combine the potatoes with the thick yogurt, cottage cheese, onion and seasonings. Carefully mix in the beaten eggs. Turn the mixture into a lightly buttered 1-quart baking dish, and top with the grated cheese mixed with the bread crumbs. Dot with small bits of butter. Bake until the top is nicely browned, about 50 to 60 minutes.

Yield: 4 to 6 servings.

**See page 16.

Spinach Pudding

2 pounds fresh spinach, or two
*   10-ounce packages frozen chopped spinach*
2 tablespoons butter
1 tablespoon minced shallots, scallions
*   or onion*
2 tablespoons flour
¾ cup yogurt
Salt and pepper to taste
1/8 to ¼ teaspoon nutmeg
Pinch of cayenne pepper (optional)
2 eggs, lightly beaten

Cook the spinach and drain it thoroughly. If using fresh spinach, chop it coarsely.

Preheat the oven to 375°.

In a heavy saucepan, melt the butter and add the minced shallots, scallions or onions. Cook them over moderate heat for a few minutes, until they are soft but not brown. Add the flour and stir until blended. Cook for a minute or two, then add the yogurt. Cook, stirring, until the sauce is thick and starting to bubble. Season with salt, pepper, nutmeg and cayenne. Mix in the spinach and remove the pan from the heat. Let the mixture cool for a minute or two, then add the beaten eggs, stirring them in well.

Butter a 4-cup baking dish and pour in the spinach mixture. Set the baking dish in a pan containing about ½ inch of hot water (which you have placed on a rack in the lower third of the oven). Bake about 35 minutes until top is slightly puffed and golden brown.

Yield: 4 servings.

Baked Acorn Squash

2 large or 4 small acorn squashes
¾ cup thick yogurt**, or ½ cup yogurt cheese**
*   mixed with ¼ cup plain yogurt*
Salt and pepper to taste
¼ teaspoon powdered ginger
1 tablespoon orange juice
1 teaspoon lemon juice
1 tablespoon butter

Cut the squash in half, scoop out the seeds and steam the squash for about 12 to 15 minutes, or until soft but not mushy. Don't let the skins fall apart.

Preheat the oven to 350°.

When the squash is cool enough to handle, carefully scoop out the pulp from the shells and mix it with the yogurt, seasonings and juices. Whip lightly with a fork or whisk to blend thoroughly, and pile the mixture back into the squash shells.

Lightly butter a shallow baking dish. Place squash halves in the dish, top with dots of butter and bake in the lower third of the oven for about 20 minutes.

Yield: 4 servings.

Note: If prepared in advance, increase the baking time to about 30 minutes, or until the squash is thoroughly heated.

**See page 16.

Baked Squash with Spinach

2 butternut or acorn squashes,
*   about 1 pound each*
1½ cups cooked chopped spinach
½ cup thick yogurt**

Salt and pepper to taste
¼ teaspoon nutmeg

Preheat the oven to 350°.

Cut the squash in half and remove the seeds. Cook the squash halves either by steaming them over boiling water in a tightly covered pot for about 12 to 15 minutes, or by baking them cut side down in a shallow baking pan, with just enough water to cover the bottom of the dish in a 350° oven for 45 minutes. Squash should be soft but not mushy.

Combine the cooked spinach with the thick yogurt, blending thoroughly. Add the salt, pepper and nutmeg.

Fill the hollows of the squash with the spinach mixture. Place the filled squash halves in a shallow baking dish, with just enough water to cover the bottom of the dish, and bake for about 30 minutes.

Yield: 4 servings.

**See page 16.

Tomatoes Stuffed with Mushrooms

4 medium-size ripe tomatoes
    (about 1½ pounds)
Salt
½ cup Duxelles (see page 161)
*½ cup thick yogurt***

Preheat the oven to 350°.

Cut off and discard the top of the tomatoes (about a third of the way down). Scoop out the insides carefully and sprinkle the shells with salt. Invert the tomatoes on a plate to drain.

Mix the Duxelles with the thick yogurt and fill the tomatoes with the mixture.

Bake for about 15 minutes or until the skin wrinkles. Serve warm or cold.

Yield: 4 servings.

**See page 16.

Baked Stuffed Zucchini

4 medium zucchini (about 1½ pounds)
*¼ cup yogurt cheese**
1 tablespoon minced parsley (preferably flat type)
½ teaspoon salt
Pepper to taste
2 tablespoons grated Parmesan cheese
2 tablespoons bread crumbs
1 to 2 tablespoons olive oil

Preheat the oven to 375°.

Scrub the zucchini and slice off the ends. Boil the zucchini in salted water for about 4 or 5 minutes. Cut each in half lengthwise and scoop out the pulp (a grapefruit spoon is good for this). Reserve the shells.

Chop and mash the zucchini pulp and mix it thoroughly with the yogurt cheese, parsley, salt and pepper.

Fill the zucchini shells with the stuffing mixture. Combine the grated cheese and bread crumbs, and spread lightly and evenly on the stuffed zucchini.

Butter a shallow baking dish that will hold the zucchini snugly and comfortably. Dribble a little olive oil over each, and bake in the upper third of the oven about 25 to 30 minutes until browned.

Yield: 4 servings.

Note: If the zucchini are large, three will do. After baking, divide each half again to give 3 pieces per serving.

**See page 16.

Shredded Zucchini

4 to 6 zucchini (about 1½ pounds)
1 cup thick yogurt**
Salt and pepper to taste
Pinch of nutmeg

Scrub the zucchini and slice off the ends. Coarsely shred the zucchini and sprinkle it with a little salt. Place in a sieve, and allow it to drain for about 30 minutes.

Place the thick yogurt in a skillet over low heat. Drain the zucchini further by squeezing it with your hands or pressing it with paper towels. Add the zucchini to the yogurt and stir well to mix. Raise the heat to moderate and cook, stirring, for about 2 or 3 minutes. Taste it and add salt (if necessary), pepper and nutmeg. Stir well and cook for another minute. Do not overcook. The zucchini should be hot and tangy and should still have some texture.

Yield: 4 to 6 servings.

**See page 16.

Eggs, Pasta
and Cheese

Eggs Baked with Cheese

4 ounces Gruyère or Cheddar cheese
  (or half of each)
4 large eggs
½ cup yogurt cream**
1 teaspoon dry mustard
½ teaspoon salt
Pinch of cayenne pepper, or freshly ground
  white pepper to taste
2 tablespoons butter

Preheat the oven to 350°.

Butter a shallow baking dish. Shred the cheese coarsely and spread it over the bottom of the dish.

Carefully break the eggs over the cheese (without breaking the yolks). Mix the yogurt cream with the mustard, salt and cayenne or white pepper, and pour the mixture over the eggs.

Dot the top with butter and bake in the lower third of the oven until the eggs are set, about 15 to 20 minutes. The yolks should remain soft, so do not overcook.

Yield: 4 servings.

**See page 16.

Mashed Potatoes with Eggs

3 cups hot mashed potatoes
1 teaspoon grated onion
Salt and pepper to taste
¼ cup yogurt cheese**
4 eggs
¼ teaspoon salt
1½ tablespoons grated sharp cheese

Preheat the oven to 350°.

Combine the mashed potatoes with the onion, salt, pepper and yogurt cheese (this can be done in a blender). Butter a shallow baking dish and spread the potato mixture in an even layer in the dish.

Make 4 hollows in the potato mixture, using a spoon or the round end of one of the eggs. Separate the eggs carefully, dropping a yolk into each of the hollows in the potato mixture.

Beat the whites with the ¼ teaspoon salt until they form soft peaks; add the grated cheese. Spread most of the whites gently over the potato mixture and egg yolks, being careful not to break the yolks. Drop about a tablespoon of whites on top of each egg to make a peak (this will help you locate the egg yolks when serving).

Bake about 10 minutes or until top is golden brown.

Yield: 4 servings.

**See page 16.

Spinach and Egg Pie

1½ pounds fresh, or two 10-ounce
*   packages frozen spinach, cooked,*
*   chopped and drained*
1 prebaked 9-inch pie shell
4 to 6 eggs
*1 cup thick yogurt**, lightly beaten*
¾ cup soft bread crumbs
3 to 4 tablespoons grated Swiss or
*   mild Cheddar cheese*
1 tablespoon melted butter

Preheat the oven to 350°.

Make sure that the spinach is very well drained; spread it evenly in the pie shell.

Make an indentation in the spinach with a large spoon for each of the eggs. Carefully break an egg into each of the indentations.

Cover the eggs carefully with a layer of beaten thick yogurt. Mix the bread crumbs and grated cheese with the melted butter, and sprinkle on the top.

Place on a rack in the lower third of the oven, and bake until the eggs are set, about 15 minutes.

Yield: 4 to 6 servings.

**See page 16.

Zucchini and Eggs

3 medium zucchini (1 pound)
½ teaspoon salt
2 tablespoons butter or oil, or a
    combination of both
Salt and pepper to taste
4 poached eggs
1 cup Mornay Sauce or Mushroom
    Cheese Sauce (see pages 160 and 162)

Preheat the oven to 400° or broil.

Scrub the zucchini and slice off the ends. Coarsely shred the zucchini and toss with the ½ teaspoon salt. Place the zucchini in a sieve, and allow it to drain for about 10 minutes. Press as much moisture out of the zucchini as you possibly can.

In a heavy skillet, heat the butter or oil and add the shredded zucchini and salt and pepper to taste. Cook and stir over moderate heat for about 3 or 4 minutes. Remove from the heat and spread it on the bottom of a shallow buttered baking dish. Make 4 indentations with the back of a large spoon and carefully place the poached eggs in the indentations. Cover with the sauce.

Either bake about 12 minutes until the top is lightly browned, or run the dish under the broiler to brown it.

Yield: 4 servings.

Chicken Manicotti Savarese

For the Manicotti

1 cup sifted all-purpose flour
  (sift before measuring)
1 cup water
4 eggs, beaten
¼ teaspoon salt

(Yield: About a dozen 6-inch manicotti.)

For the Filling

1½ cups finely chopped or ground cooked chicken
2 tablespoons grated Parmesan cheese
1 tablespoon minced parsley (preferably flat-leaf)
¾ cup thick yogurt**
¼ cup Duxelles (see page 161)
½ teaspoon salt
¼ teaspoon nutmeg
Pepper to taste
2 cups Sauce Mornay (see page 160)

Mix all ingredients for the manicotti either in a blender or by hand, and let the batter rest for at least 2 hours.

Mix the chicken with the grated cheese, parsley, thick yogurt, Duxelles, salt, nutmeg and pepper. The mixture should be slightly firm and able to hold its shape, but not dry and stiff. Add a bit more yogurt if necessary to soften it slightly.

If serving immediately, preheat the oven to 350°.

Make the manicotti like crepes. Brush a skillet or a 6-inch crepe pan (No. 20) with peanut or vegetable oil or clarified butter and heat over moderately high heat until the pan is very hot.

Remove pan from heat, pour 2 tablespoons of batter into the center of the pan and quickly tilt the pan so that the batter covers the entire surface.

Return the pan to the heat and cook the manicotti for about 30 seconds or until the bottom is light brown. Flip the manicotti over and cook it for about 20 seconds more. This second side will be rather spotty looking and is the side the filling is placed on.

The cooked manicotti can be placed on a clean tea towel or stacked with wax paper between them.

Note: A standard coffee measure is a very easy way to measure the batter.

To speed up the process use 2 pans. The second pan can be any size skillet as the manicotti is already formed. When the first side of the manicotti is cooked, flip it into the second pan to cook the other side and start cooking the next manicotti in the first pan.

Advance Preparation: The manicotti can be made in advance and refrigerated for about 2 days.

Spoon a lightly rounded tablespoon of the filling on the center of each, fold the top third down over the filling and fold the bottom third up and over the top third (like a business letter). Be sure the spotty side (the second cooked side) is the one you place the filling on.

Place the filled manicotti side by side, seam side down, in a lightly buttered shallow baking dish. Spoon the Mornay Sauce evenly over the manicotti. Place the dish in the upper third of the oven. Bake until light brown and bubbling, about 25 or 30 minutes.

Yield: 4 servings (as a main course) or 6 servings (as a first course).

**See page 16.

Linguine with Pesto

2 cups chopped fresh basil leaves (see Note)
1 cup chopped fresh Italian (flat-leaf) parsley
½ cup grated Parmesan cheese
¼ cup grated Romano cheese
1 clove garlic
1 tablespoon pignoli (pine) nuts
12 blanched almonds or walnut halves
2 tablespoons yogurt cheese**
2 tablespoons yogurt
3 tablespoons softened butter
1½ pounds linguine (or other pasta)

Puree all ingredients except the pasta in a blender until perfectly smooth. Transfer contents to a small bowl and place the bowl in a pan (or another bowl) containing very hot water. It is not necessary to heat the pesto (green sauce) by cooking.

Cook the pasta according to package directions. When the pasta is almost ready to serve, scald a large serving bowl with very hot water and dry it. Place the pesto in the bottom of the bowl.

Drain the pasta, but save about 4 tablespoons of the cooking water. Toss the pasta with the pesto in the bowl. Add the 4 tablespoons cooking water and toss again.

Yield 4 to 6 servings.

Note: If fresh basil is out of season, substitute 2 cups of fresh spinach for the basil.

Pesto is also delicious in soups or tossed with hot rice.

**See page 16.

Baked Stuffed Shells

24 jumbo (no. 95) pasta shells (about 6 ounces)
¾ cup cooked, chopped spinach
¾ cup yogurt cheese**
6 ounces mozzarella cheese, shredded or diced
½ cup grated Parmesan cheese
1 egg, beaten
¼ teaspoon nutmeg
½ teaspoon salt
Pepper to taste
2 cups basic Tomato Sauce (see page 166)
¼ cup grated Parmesan cheese (optional)

Preheat the oven to 350°.

Cook the shells in a large quantity of boiling salted water according to package directions (usually about 10 minutes). Do not overcook.

While the shells are cooking, mix together the chopped spinach, yogurt cheese, mozzarella and Parmesan. Add the egg and mix thoroughly. Blend in the nutmeg and add salt and pepper.

Select a shallow baking dish that will accommodate the shells in 1 layer (a rectangular dish about 8½" x 10½" or an oval dish about 12" x 7½"). Cover the bottom of the dish with about 2/3 cup of the tomato sauce.

Drain the shells as soon as they are cooked, and, while they are still warm, fill each with about a tablespoon of the spinach-and-cheese mixture. Place the shells in the baking dish. They should fit comfortably, touching one another. Spread the rest of the sauce evenly over the shells.

Bake about 30 minutes or until bubbling. Serve with a bowl of additional grated Parmesan, if desired.

Yield: 4 to 6 servings.

**See page 16.

Rice and Mushroom Pie

4 cups cooked rice
2 tablespoons butter
½ pound mushrooms, sliced
1 small onion, minced
1 teaspoon lemon juice
½ teaspoon salt (or to taste)
Pepper to taste
Pinch of nutmeg
2 teaspoons cornstarch
2 teaspoons water
1 cup yogurt
1/3 cup shredded Gruyere or other mild cheese

Preheat the oven to 350°.

Butter a shallow baking dish or pie plate, and spread half of the rice on the bottom of the dish.

In a heavy skillet, melt the butter and sauté the mushrooms and onion over moderate heat until they are tender, about 4 or 5 minutes. Add the lemon juice, salt, pepper and nutmeg. Spread the mushrooms, onion and their juices evenly on top of the rice.

Make a paste of the cornstarch and water and put it in the skillet with the yogurt over moderate heat. Stir until the sauce is hot and bubbling. Taste and adjust seasonings.

Spread half the sauce over the mushroom-and-onion layer and sprinkle with half the cheese. Cover this with the balance of the rice, smoothing it with the back of a spoon. Top with the rest of the sauce and sprinkle with the remaining cheese.

Bake until the top is lightly browned, about 30 to 35 minutes.

Yield: 6 servings.

VARIATION

Substitute cooked cubed meat or tuna fish for the filling.

Herb Cheese Quiche

3 large eggs
1 cup yogurt
¼ teaspoon salt
Pepper to taste
Pinch of nutmeg
½ cup yogurt cheese**
¼ cup cottage cheese
2 tablespoons minced chives, or 1 tablespoon minced scallion
   stems
1 tablespoon minced parsley
1 prebaked 8- or 9-inch pie shell
1½ tablespoons butter

Preheat the oven to 375°.

Beat together the eggs, yogurt, salt, pepper and nutmeg.

In a separate bowl, mix the yogurt cheese with the cottage cheese and herbs.

Spread the cheese-and-herb mixture in the prebaked pie shell. Pour the egg-and-yogurt mixture over this and dot the top with bits of butter.

Bake in the upper third of the oven until set, about 30 to 35 minutes.

Yield: 4 to 6 servings.

**See page 16.

Mushroom Quiche

2 tablespoons butter or oil, or a combination of both
½ pound mushrooms, sliced thinly
Salt and pepper to taste
Few drops lemon juice
1 prebaked 8- or 9-inch pie shell
3 large eggs
1 cup yogurt
¼ teaspoon salt
Pinch of nutmeg
½ cup yogurt cheese**
¼ cup cottage cheese
1½ tablespoons butter

Preheat the oven to 375°.

In a heavy pan, heat the 2 tablespoons butter or oil and sauté the mushrooms over moderately high heat for about 4 or 5 minutes. Sprinkle with salt and pepper to taste and the lemon juice. The mushrooms should be almost dry. Strew the mushrooms over the bottom of the baked pie shell.

Beat together the eggs, yogurt, salt, pepper to taste and the nutmeg.

In a separate bowl, mix the yogurt cheese and cottage cheese. Spread this mixture over the mushrooms in the pie shell. Pour the egg-and-yogurt mixture over, and dot the top with the 1½ tablespoons butter, cut into small bits.

Bake in the upper third of the oven until set, about 30 to 35 minutes.

Yield: 4 to 6 servings.

**See page 16.

Cauliflower Souffle

1 medium head cauliflower (about 1½ pounds)
    or two 10-ounce packages frozen cauliflower
2 medium or 3 small potatoes, (½ pound)
    boiled and peeled
4 tablespoons butter
½ cup thick yogurt**
3 eggs, separated, plus 1 extra egg white
    (at room temperature)
Salt and pepper to taste
¼ teaspoon nutmeg
Pinch of paprika
2 teaspoons prepared horseradish, drained
¼ teaspoon cream of tartar
1 tablespoon bread crumbs mixed with
1 tablespoon grated Parmesan or Cheddar cheese

If using fresh cauliflower, trim the leaves and cut off the stem (save the stem and leaves for soups or Green Vegetable Dip—see page 20), and soak the florets in cold water for about 15 minutes. Cook them in boiling salted water for about 15 minutes, until they are soft. If using frozen cauliflower, cook according to package directions. Drain the cauliflower thoroughly and return it to the pan. Shake the pan over moderate heat, tossing the cauliflower lightly to thoroughly dry it.

Preheat the oven to 400°.

In a food mill or blender, puree the cauliflower and potatoes and beat in the butter, thick yogurt and egg yolks. Add seasonings and blend briefly.

Butter a 6-cup soufflé dish. Sprinkle 1 tablespoon of the bread crumbs and grated cheese on the bottom and sides and turn the dish to coat it with the crumb mixture. Shake out any excess crumbs.

Beat the egg whites with a pinch of salt until they become foamy. Add the cream of tartar and continue beating until the whites form peaks. Stir about a third of the egg whites into the pureed vegetable mixture. Fold in the rest of the whites quickly and lightly.

Turn the mixture into the dish and top with the remaining bread crumbs and grated cheese.

Place in the lower third of the oven, immediately lower the temperature to 375° and bake until set, about 40 minutes.

Yield: 4 servings.

Note: Most soufflé recipes call for attaching a strip of buttered aluminum foil around the top of the dish to form a collar about 3 inches high. This is in order to contain the puff when the soufflé rises. You can do it for this to be on the safe side, but you will find that this soufflé has more body and will not rise as much as other soufflés.

**See page 16.

Cheese Souffle

4 tablespoons butter
1 tablespoon grated Swiss or Parmesan cheese
3 tablespoons flour
1 cup yogurt, lightly beaten
Salt and pepper to taste
Pinch of nutmeg
Pinch of cayenne pepper
4 eggs plus 1 extra egg white
    (all at room temperature)
¼ teaspoon cream of tartar (optional)
¾ cup grated Swiss or Parmesan cheese,
    or a combination of both

Rub 1 tablespoon of the butter all over the inside of a 6-cup soufflé dish and sprinkle 1 tablespoon of grated cheese on the soufflé dish, rolling it around to coat the bottom and sides.

Shake out excess.

Preheat the oven to 400°.

In a large heavy pan, melt the remaining 3 tablespoons butter. Stir in the flour and blend well with a wooden spoon. Cook the mixture over moderate heat for a few minutes until it is foamy but not brown. Remove the pan from the heat and add the beaten yogurt. Stir with a wire whisk and return the pan to the heat. Continue stirring until the mixture is very thick, smooth and bubbling. Blend in the seasonings and cook for a minute.

Remove the pan from the heat. Separate the eggs, dropping the whites into a bowl and adding the yolks to the sauce in the pan. Beat the sauce after each addition. Taste and adjust seasonings.

Add the extra egg white to the four in the bowl, and beat them with a pinch of salt. If you do not have an unlined copper bowl you will need the cream of tartar to stabilize the whites. Add it after you have been beating the whites for about 30 seconds. Beat the egg whites until they are stiff. Stir about a quarter of them into the sauce base to lighten it. Then fold in the rest of the egg whites, stirring in all but a tablespoon of the ¾ cup grated cheese while folding. Work quickly so as not to deflate the egg whites.

Pour the mixture into the soufflé dish. Butter a long strip of aluminum foil (about 4 inches wide) and wrap it around the top of the soufflé dish to make a collar that will stick up 3 inches above the soufflé dish. Pin it in place with 2 straight pins.

Place the soufflé in the lower third of the oven. Immediately lower the temperature to 375°. Do not open the oven door for 30 minutes. At that time, the top should be puffy and golden. Quickly sprinkle the top with the reserved tablespoon of cheese and cook the soufflé for about 5 or 6 minutes more. Serve immediately.

Yield: 2 to 4 servings.

VARIATIONS

Reduce the cheese to about 1/3 to ½ cup, and add ¾ cup chopped cooked spinach, spinach and Duxelles (see page 161), or spinach with a little bit of minced ham or chicken.

Salads and
Salad Dressings

Mixed Salads

A B C SALAD

Combine equal parts of diced, peeled apples with shredded or diced cooked beets and sliced or diced cucumbers (which have been salted and allowed to drain for about 20 minutes). Toss with yogurt and salt and pepper, or a dressing of your choice.

BEETS

Toss sliced, diced or shredded cooked beets with yogurt and a bit of minced onion or horseradish. Season with salt and pepper.

CARROTS

Toss shredded raw carrots with a little lemon juice or a combination of lemon and orange juice. Add just a bit of grated fresh ginger or a pinch of powdered ginger. Let the carrots marinate for several hours, tossing them occasionally. Mix well with thick yogurt** and serve.

CELERY AND RAW MUSHROOMS

Combine equal parts of diced celery and sliced raw mushrooms. Sprinkle with lemon juice, salt and pepper, and toss with yogurt.

ENDIVE AND WATERCRESS

Slice Belgian endive heads crosswise in ½-inch slices. Toss with about twice as much watercress and just enough Vinaigrette Dressing (see page 157) to coat the greens.

MUSHROOMS

Raw mushrooms are a wonderful addition to a salad. If you are adding them to a plain green salad, let mushroom slices marinate very briefly in the salad dressing before adding them to the greens. Possible combinations with sliced raw mushrooms might include:
- Diced ham, cubed cooked potatoes and cooked green beans with Mustard Dressing (see page 157).

- Tuna or salmon chunks, cooked green peas, sliced raw zucchini, onion rings and Curry Dressing (see page 156).

**See page 16.

- A varied assortment of greens, julienne strips of cheese, ham, tongue, chicken, turkey, etc. Add a few capers to Vinaigrette Dressing (see page 157) and toss well.

- Diced chicken, water chestnuts and celery. Mix yogurt with mayonnaise, add salt and pepper and toss.

- Fresh spinach leaves, coarsely shredded, and crumbled bacon or chopped walnuts. Toss with Vinaigrette Dressing (see page 157) to coat lightly.

STUFFED TOMATOES

Wash ripe tomatoes, remove the caps, scoop out the pulp and sprinkle the insides with salt. Invert the tomatoes to drain briefly. Fill them with:

●Tuna fish or salmon mixed with minced onion, chopped celery, thick yogurt**, salt and pepper. Serve on lettuce leaves with a mixture of yogurt and mayonnaise.

●Thick yogurt** combined with chopped radishes, cubed, peeled cucumbers (which have been salted and drained for about 20 minutes) and chopped chives or minced parsley. Top with yogurt seasoned with salt and pepper.

VEGETABLE SALAD

Combine cooked vegetables, minced onion or scallions and minced parsley with a dressing composed of 1/3 mayonnaise and 2/3 yogurt, seasoned with salt and pepper, or use Curry or Mustard Dressing (see pages 156 and 157). Suggested vegetables to combine include:

Diced cooked carrots	Cooked peas
Cubed cooked potatoes	Chopped celery, cooked or raw
Cut-up cooked string beans	Cooked lima beans

**See page 16.

Apple and Celery Salad

¾ cup drained yogurt**
2 large apples
3 or 4 stalks celery
Black pepper to taste
Salt to taste
Lettuce leaves

Place the drained yogurt in a mixing bowl.

Core and peel the apples and dice them quickly (there should be about 2 cups). Put them in the bowl with the yogurt.

Chop the celery (there should be about 2 cups) and add them to the bowl. Add freshly ground black pepper and salt and toss well.

Serve on lettuce leaves.

Yield: 4 to 6 servings.

**See page 16.

Avocado Stuffed with Cottage Cheese

1 small cucumber
8 medium radishes (about ½ cup), chopped
1 cup drained yogurt**
1 cup cottage cheese
1 tablespoon lemon juice or
white wine vinegar
½ to 1 teaspoon salt
Pepper to taste
2 tablespoons minced chives or
scallion stems
2 ripe avocados (medium)
Lemon half or wedge
Lettuce leaves

Peel the cucumber, split it lengthwise and scoop out the seeds with the tip of a spoon. Chop it coarsely (there should be ½ cup) and toss it with a little salt. Let the cucumber drain for about 30 minutes in a sieve. Chop the radishes and set them aside in cold water to cover.

Mix together the drained yogurt, cottage cheese, lemon juice or vinegar, salt, pepper and minced chives or scallion stems. Add the drained cucumbers and the radishes (patted dry with a paper towel), and blend gently.

Cut the avocados in half lengthwise, remove the pits and rub the cut surfaces with the lemon to prevent discoloration. Fill the avocado halves with the yogurt-and-cottage cheese mixture and serve on lettuce leaves.

Yield: 4 servings.

**See page 16.

Minted Green Bean Salad

1½ pounds fresh green beans or two
    10-ounce packages frozen green beans
*1 cup drained yogurt***
1 clove garlic, minced
1 tablespoon minced fresh mint
    or ½ teaspoon dried mint
1 tablespoon minced parsley (preferably flat-leaf),
    or 1 tablespoon minced fresh coriander
½ teaspoon basil
Salt to taste
¼ teaspoon black pepper

Cook the beans until they are barely tender. Drain them and press out the excess water.

In a bowl, combine the drained yogurt and the garlic, mint, parsley or coriander, basil, salt and pepper. Beat together gently.

Toss with the green beans and refrigerate for several hours or overnight.

Yield: 4 to 6 servings.

**See page 16.

Cheese Salad

6 ounces Gruyère cheese
1½ cups cooked ham
1½ cups sliced or diced cooked carrots
Salt and pepper to taste
1 tablespoon wine vinegar
1 tablespoon Dijon-type mustard
*½ cup drained yogurt***
¼ cup mayonnaise
Lettuce leaves

Cut the Gruyère and the ham into julienne strips.

Sprinkle the carrots with a little salt and pepper.

Blend together the vinegar, mustard, drained yogurt and mayonnaise. Taste and adjust seasonings. Toss the cheese, ham and carrots with the dressing. Serve as a side dish on lettuce leaves.

Yield: 4 to 6 servings.

**See page 16.

Country Salad

8 ounces Swiss cheese, cubed
2 cups cubed cooked potatoes
6 hard-boiled eggs, coarsely chopped
1 cup pickled beets, drained
1 cup cut-up cooked green beans
1 cup drained yogurt**
1/3 cup mayonnaise
1 tablespoon lemon juice
1 tablespoon minced fresh dill
Salt and pepper to taste

Place cheese cubes, potato cubes, chopped eggs, beets and beans in a serving bowl.

In another bowl, combine the drained yogurt, mayonnaise, lemon juice, dill, salt and pepper. Mix well to blend. Pour over the cheese and vegetables and toss to coat thoroughly.

Yield: 4 to 6 servings.

**See page 16.

Basic Coleslaw

1 pound cabbage (½ medium head)
1 cup drained yogurt**
1 tablespoon sugar or honey
1 tablespoon wine vinegar
1 teaspoon salt
1 teaspoon freshly ground pepper

Shred the cabbage finely.

Blend all the other ingredients together and toss with the shredded cabbage. Let stand for at least an hour, tossing once or twice.

Cover and refrigerate for several hours.

Toss well before serving.

Yield: 6 servings.

VARIATIONS

Any or all of the following would go very well mixed with the shredded cabbage:

Grated or shredded carrots

Diced green or red peppers

Diced celery

**See page 16.

Minced scallions or red onion

Few tablespoons minced parsley

About 1 teaspoon caraway or celery seeds

Chicken and Artichoke Salad

3 cups large cubes of cooked chicken
One 8½-ounce can artichoke hearts, well drained,
*   or one 9-ounce package frozen artichoke hearts,*
*   cooked, drained and cooled*
12 toasted almonds
*½ cup thick yogurt***
½ cup mayonnaise
1 tablespoon lemon juice
Salt and pepper to taste
Lettuce leaves (preferably Boston or
*   other soft lettuce)*
12 black olives

Combine the chicken with the artichoke hearts and the almonds.

Mix together the thick yogurt and mayonnaise and add the lemon juice, salt and pepper. Blend well. Taste and adjust seasonings.

Toss the chicken and artichoke hearts gently with the dressing, coating the chicken and artichokes evenly.

Either line a shallow bowl with lettuce leaves and heap the chicken salad in the center or serve on individual plates on a bed of lettuce. Garnish with black olives.

Yield: 4 servings.

**See page 16.

Cucumbers with Yogurt

2 medium cucumbers (about 1½ pounds)
*½ cup thick yogurt***
1 clove garlic, minced
2 tablespoons oil
Salt and pepper to taste
2 tablespoons minced flat-leaf parsley,
    or 2 tablespoons chopped fresh chives
Black olives and radishes

Peel the cucumbers and cut them in half lengthwise. Scoop out the seeds with the tip of a spoon. Cut the cucumbers into small cubes (there should be about 3 cups), sprinkle with a little salt and let them drain for about 30 minutes in a sieve.

In another bowl, combine the thick yogurt with the garlic and oil, mixing gently but thoroughly. Add the drained cucumbers and stir gently. Taste and add salt and pepper and the parsley or chives. Chill for an hour or so before serving. Garnish with black olives and radishes.

Yield: 4 servings.

**See page 16.

Cucumber Salad

2 small or 1 large cucumber (about 1½ pounds)
2 tablespoons chopped fresh mint
1 tablespoon lemon juice
1 clove garlic, minced
Salt and pepper to taste
1 cup drained yogurt**
6 radishes, sliced
6 scallions

Scrub the cucumbers and slice them thinly. There should be about 3 cups. Do not peel unless they are waxed. Toss the slices with some salt and let them drain in a sieve for about 30 minutes. Pat them dry with paper towels.

Mix the mint, lemon juice, garlic, salt and pepper, and blend well with the drained yogurt. Taste and adjust seasonings.

Arrange the cucumber slices on a plate and pour the yogurt sauce over them. Garnish with the sliced radishes and scallions.

Yield: 6 servings.

**See page 16.

Fruit Salad

2 ripe cantaloupes
2 cups seedless grapes
2 oranges, peeled and cut up
¾ cup thick yogurt**
1 tablespoon honey
1 teaspoon lemon juice (or to taste)
Salt to taste
Pinch of curry powder or pepper (optional)
Lettuce leaves

Quarter the cantaloupes and scoop out the seeds. Cut the fruit away from the rind, then cut into large cubes. Combine the cantaloupe, grapes and oranges.

Combine the thick yogurt, honey, lemon juice and salt, and beat well. Taste and adjust seasonings. Add the curry powder or pepper.

Toss the fruit with the dressing so that it is lightly coated. Let the fruit and dressing macerate for about 30 minutes in the refrigerator before serving on lettuce leaves.

Yield: 6 to 8 servings.

Note: If you have fresh mint, mince a little and sprinkle it on the top.

**See page 16.

Green Pea Mousse

1 cup boiling water or boiling vegetable water
1 envelope unflavored gelatin
2 cups cooked peas
½ teaspoon salt
1/8 teaspoon white pepper
Pinch of chervil
*1 cup thick yogurt***

Put the boiling water (or water the peas cooked in) and the gelatin into the container of a blender and blend at high speed for 40 seconds. Add the peas, salt, pepper and chervil. Cover and blend for another 40 seconds at high speed. Remove the cover and, with the motor running, add the thick yogurt. Taste and adjust seasonings, and pour the mixture into a 3-cup mold. Chill until firm, about 2 hours.

Yield: 4 servings.

**See page 16.

Potato Salad

6 to 8 new potatoes (3 pounds)
2/3 cup drained yogurt**
1/3 cup mayonnaise
½ cup finely chopped celery
½ cup finely chopped onion or scallions
½ cup chopped green or red peppers
¼ cup minced parsley (preferably flat-leaf)
Salt and pepper to taste
Lettuce leaves (optional)
Black olives, pimiento strips and capers

Wash the potatoes but do not peel them. Put them in boiling water to cover and add just a pinch of salt. Cook them until they are just barely done (test with a fork), about 20 or 25 minutes.

Mix the drained yogurt with the mayonnaise.

When the potatoes are done, drain them and run cold water over them. Don't let them stand in the cold water. You want them just cool enough to handle. Peel the potatoes and either slice them or cut them into small cubes. Place the potatoes in a large bowl and add the chopped vegetables, parsley and the dressing, tossing gently but thoroughly to mix. Season with salt and pepper as you toss.

Refrigerate briefly before serving. Serve in a salad bowl or on a platter lined with lettuce leaves, if you like. Garnish with black olives, pimiento strips and possibly capers.

Note: Although you can use all-purpose potatoes, the texture of new potatoes is much better, and they will hold their shape.

Yield: 6 servings.

**See page 16.

Rice Salad

2 cups cooked rice (preferably hot)
One 10-ounce package frozen mixed
    vegetables, cooked and drained
¼ cup chopped celery
¼ cup chopped green pepper
Salt and pepper to taste
2/3 cup thick yogurt**
1/3 cup·mayonnaise
¼ cup minced parsley
1 teaspoon curry powder (or to taste)

Mix the rice with the mixed vegetables, celery and green pepper, tossing lightly with salt and pepper.

Mix together the thick yogurt, mayonnaise, parsley and curry powder; blend well.

Add the dressing to the rice and vegetables and toss well to coat with the dressing. Refrigerate for 1 or 2 hours before serving.

Yield: 4 servings

**See page 16.

Blue Cheese Dressing

½ cup yogurt
2½ ounces blue cheese, crumbled
1 teaspoon wine vinegar
1 tablespoon chopped chives or
    minced shallots
¼ teaspoon black pepper

Blend all ingredients well. Chill before serving on mixed green or raw spinach salad.

Yield: 1 cup.

Caraway Cottage Cheese Dressing

2 chopped radishes
2 hard-boiled egg yolks, mashed
1 clove garlic, minced
1 tablespoon minced green pepper
½ cup cottage cheese
½ cup drained yogurt**
1 to 2 tablespoons lemon juice
1 teaspoon salt
1 teaspoon caraway seeds
½ teaspoon paprika

Combine all the ingredients and mix thoroughly. Chill briefly and serve on a green salad.

Yield: 1 1/3 cups.

**See page 16.

Cottage Cheese Dressing

1 cup cottage cheese
1 cup yogurt
1 to 2 tablespoons lemon juice or
    white wine vinegar
1 clove garlic, crushed
1 tablespoon minced chives
½ teaspoon salt
Pepper to taste

Puree the cottage cheese in a blender or by forcing it through a sieve. Add the other ingredients and blend well. Chill briefly before serving.

Yield: 2 cups.

Curry Dressing

1 cup drained yogurt**
1/3 cup mayonnaise
1 tablespoon minced scallions or shallots
1 to 2 teaspoons lemon juice
1 to 2 teaspoons curry powder
½ teaspoon salt

Blend all ingredients thoroughly. Chill before serving. Try it on cold fish as well as on a raw spinach or mixed green salad.

Yield: 1 1/3 cups.

**See page 16.

Dill Dressing

1 cup drained yogurt**
1 tablespoon minced onion
1 tablespoon minced fresh dill or
   1½ teaspoons dried dill
Salt and pepper to taste

Blend all the ingredients well. Chill briefly before serving. Very good for shrimp or salmon or with cold potatoes. If using on fish, a garnish of a few capers would be nice.

**See page 16.

Yield: 1 cup.

Honey Dressing

1 cup thick yogurt**
1 tablespoon honey
2 teaspoons grated orange rind

Blend all the ingredients well and chill briefly before serving. Very good for fruit salads.

Yield: 1 cup.

**See page 16.

Mustard Dressing

2/3 cup drained yogurt**
1/3 cup mayonnaise
2 teaspoons Dijon-type mustard (or to taste)

Blend all ingredients thoroughly several hours before you wish to serve. Refrigerate until serving time.

**See page 16.

Yield: 1 cup.

Vinaigrette Dressing

½ teaspoon Dijon-type mustard
¼ cup wine vinegar
½ cup drained yogurt**
½ cup olive or salad oil
½ teaspoon salt (or to taste)
¼ teaspoon pepper (or to taste)

Dissolve the mustard in the vinegar, then add the remaining ingredients. A blender does a good job of thoroughly mixing all the ingredients (or you can use a wire whisk). This is a good basic dressing for mixed green, raw spinach or chef salads.

Note: Add a clove of crushed garlic or, for a more delicate garlic flavoring, let 1 or 2 split peeled garlic cloves sit in the olive oil for several hours. Discard garlic.

Yield: 1¼ cups.

**See page 16.

Sauces

Basic White (Béchamel) Sauce

2 tablespoons butter
3 tablespoons flour
2 cups yogurt, or 1 cup milk and
   1 cup yogurt
Salt and pepper to taste

In a heavy pan, melt the butter over moderate heat. Add the flour and stir to blend. Stirring slowly, cook over moderate heat until the butter and flour foam together. Let the roux cook for about 2 minutes, but do not brown.

Remove the pan from the heat and let the butter and flour stop bubbling. If you are using all yogurt, add a little yogurt to the roux and blend it in with a wire whisk. Add a little more yogurt and return the pan to moderate heat. Continue adding the yogurt, blending it in with a wire whisk. Bring the sauce to a slow boil, stirring slowly, and cook it for about 2 minutes. Add the salt and pepper and stir for a minute. Taste and adjust seasonings.

If you are using milk and yogurt, heat the milk almost to the boil. Remove the pan containing the roux from the heat and let it stop bubbling. Add the hot milk all at once, beating well with a wire whisk to blend it in smoothly. With a spoon or spatula, scrape around the inside of the pan to make sure you have incorporated all the roux. Then return the pan to the heat and add the yogurt, whisking to blend it in. When the sauce has reached a boil, season it. Taste and adjust seasonings.

Yield: 2 cups.

Mornay Sauce

2 cups Basic White (Béchamel) Sauce
(see page 159)
¼ to ½ cup coarsely grated Swiss cheese, or
half Swiss and half finely grated Parmesan cheese
Salt and pepper to taste
Pinch of cayenne pepper (optional)
Pinch of nutmeg (preferably freshly ground)

Bring the white sauce to the boil. Remove the pan from the heat and beat in the grated cheese until it is melted and blended into the sauce. Add seasonings to taste.

Yield: 2 cups.

Curry Sauce

1 tablespoon butter
½ cup minced onion
2 tablespoons curry powder (or to taste)
Ingredients for Basic White (Béchamel) Sauce
(see page 159)
Few drops lemon juice (optional)

In a heavy pan, melt the butter over medium low heat and cook the onion until soft and wilted. Add the curry powder and cook for a few minutes, stirring. Then add the additional butter, flour, yogurt, salt and pepper exactly as outlined in the Basic White Sauce recipe. After the sauce has reached the boil, taste and adjust seasonings and add the lemon juice.

Yield: 2 cups.

Cream of Tomato Sauce

2 cups Basic White (Béchamel) Sauce
(see page 159)
3 to 4 tablespoons tomato paste

When the white sauce has reached the boil, add the tomato paste gradually, stirring and simmering long enough to blend.

Note: See page 166 for Basic Tomato Sauce.

Yield: 2 cups.

Duxelles

½ pound mushrooms, very finely chopped
3 tablespoons butter or oil, or a
*   combination of both*
2 tablespoons minced shallots or scallions
Salt and pepper to taste
¼ cup Madeira or port, or ¼ cup brown stock

There should be about 2 cups of finely chopped mushrooms. Squeeze them, over a small bowl a handful at a time, in the corner of a clean tea towel to extract the juices. (Save the juices for seasoning in other cooking.) Or put the mushrooms through a ricer to press out the juice.

In a large heavy pan, melt the butter or oil. Saute the shallots or scallions and mushrooms over moderately high heat, stirring them. The mushrooms will start to separate and give up the rest of their juices. This should take about 6 or 7 minutes. Add the salt and pepper. Add the wine or stock and raise the heat slightly to ᵃte it. Remove from heat.

Yield out 1½ cups.

Mushroom Sauce

½ cup Duxelles (see page 161)
½ cup thick yogurt**
1 teaspoon minced parsley

Heat the Duxelles briefly, add the thick yogurt and parsley and heat. Do not let the sauce boil.
Note: The basis for many sauces is a minced mushroom mixture called Duxelles. It will keep under refrigeration for several weeks and can also be frozen. Its uses are varied: sauces, soups, soufflés, stews, stuffings, crepes, quiches, omelets, etc.

Yield: 1 cup.

**See page 16.

Mushroom Cream Sauce

1 clove garlic
3 tablespoons butter
3 tablespoons minced onion
2 tablespoons flour
1 cup yogurt
½ pound mushrooms, thinly sliced
¼ cup dry vermouth, dry white wine,
*   sherry or water*
Salt and pepper to taste
Pinch of nutmeg

In a heavy pan, cook the garlic in 2 tablespoons of the butter for about 1 minute. Discard the garlic. Add the onion to the pan and cook it over moderate heat for about 2 or 3 minutes, until soft but not brown. Add the flour and stir well to blend. Cook over moderate heat for a minute or so. Add the yogurt gradually, stirring to blend, until the mixture comes to a boil. Remove from the heat and set aside.

In another pan, melt the remaining tablespoon of butter and add the sliced mushrooms. Add the wine or water and a little salt and pepper. Cook the mushrooms for about 5 minutes or so, until practically all of the liquid is evaporated.

Add the mushrooms to the sauce base and return to the heat. Cook, stirring, over very low heat for about 5 minutes. Add the nutmeg; taste and adjust seasonings. Simmer for a few more minutes.

Yield: About 2 cups.

VARIATION

Add about 1/3 cup coarsely grated Gruyère or Swiss cheese and 1/3 cup finely grated Parmesan cheese to the above sauce after removing it from the heat.

Dill Sauce

2 tablespoons butter
2 tablespoons flour
½ cup hot beef broth
1 tablespoon wine vinegar
1 tablespoon chopped fresh dill,
*   or 1½ teaspoons dried dill*
½ teaspoon sugar
½ teaspoon salt
½ cup thick yogurt**

In a heavy pan, melt the butter, stir in the flour and cook them together over moderate heat until the mixture colors very slightly.

Remove from heat and beat in the beef broth and vinegar, and add the dill, sugar and salt. Blend with a wire whisk and return the pan to the heat. Simmer for 2 or 3 minutes, stirring occasionally. Lower the heat, blend in the thick yogurt and heat briefly. Serve with hot or cold meat.

Yield: 1½ cups.

**See page 16.

Mustard Sauce

1½ tablespoons Dijon-type mustard
¾ cup drained yogurt**
1 cup beef broth
1 tablespoon cornstarch, mixed with
    1 tablespoon dry vermouth or dry white wine
Salt and pepper to taste
1 tablespoon minced parsley

Blend the mustard with the drained yogurt and set aside.

In a small pan, heat the broth and beat in the yogurt-and-mustard mixture. Cook over low heat; do not allow it to boil. Add the cornstarch-and-wine mixture, stirring to blend well. Cook, stirring, over low heat. Add salt and pepper. Add parsley before serving.

Yield: 1¾ cups.

**See page 16.

Hollandaise Sauce

2 large egg yolks
1/3 cup thick yogurt**
1 to 2 tablespoons lemon juice
¼ teaspoon salt
Pinch of white pepper
Pinch of cayenne pepper (optional)

Beat the egg yolks lightly and beat in the remaining ingredients. Place the mixture in the top of a double boiler over hot water, or in a ceramic bowl set on a trivet in a pan containing hot water. Over moderate heat, stir the ingredients until the eggs have thickened and the sauce is very warm. Do not let the sauce boil. Serve the sauce warm, stirring it gently just before serving.

Yield: 1 cup.

VARIATION

Beat 1 egg white until it is fairly stiff. Fold the egg white into the sauce after the sauce has thickened. Stir gently. This increases the yield to about 1½ cups.

Note: This sauce can be refrigerated and reheated in a bowl set in hot water or in a double boiler over hot water.

**See page 16.

Bearnaise Sauce

¼ *cup wine vinegar*
¼ *cup dry white wine or dry vermouth*
1 tablespoon minced shallots or scallions
1 tablespoon minced fresh tarragon, or
    ½ *tablespoon dried tarragon*
1/8 teaspoon pepper
Pinch of salt
Ingredients for Hollandaise Sauce
    (see page 164)

In a small pan, combine all the ingredients except the ingredients for Hollandaise Sauce. Bring to a boil and reduce to 2 tablespoons. Strain the liquid and substitute it for the lemon juice in the Hollandaise Sauce recipe. Omit the salt and pepper from the Hollandaise Sauce recipe.

Yield: 1 cup.

Basic Tomato Sauce

No yogurt in this sauce, but it is used in the Moussaka (see page 96) and in the Baked Stuffed Shells (see page 135). Any extra sauce can be frozen—it is very useful to have on hand.

2 pounds very ripe fresh plum tomatoes,
*   or one 35-ounce can Italian plum tomatoes*
2 tablespoons olive oil
2 cloves of garlic, split
½ cup minced onion (see Note)
1½ tablespoons minced fresh basil,
*   or 1½ teaspoons dried basil*
½ teaspoon salt
½ teaspoon freshly ground black pepper
Tiny pinch of sugar

If using fresh tomatoes, peel, seed and dice them (you can put them through a food mill or a sieve to remove the seeds, which give a bitter taste). If using canned tomatoes, put them through a food mill or sieve.

In a large heavy pan, heat the olive oil and add the split garlic cloves. Sauté over low heat until the garlic is barely colored. Discard the garlic. (If by any chance the garlic burns, discard the oil and start all over again, rather than ruin the sauce.) Add the minced onion and sauté gently until it is soft and wilted but not brown. Add the tomatoes along with the basil, salt, pepper and sugar. Cook over low heat, stirring, until the sauce comes to a boil. Let it simmer for a few minutes, then raise the heat to moderate and cook, stirring occasionally, for about 30 minutes. Taste and adjust the seasonings. The sauce should be nice and thick with body and flavor, and the excess liquid of the tomatoes should be evaporated. If not, cook longer.

Yield: 3½ cups.

Note: For some dishes, you may wish to eliminate the onions. For a rich, thick sauce (sometimes called a coulis or fondue) use the onions, and add a piece of orange peel, some fennel seeds and a tablespoon of tomato paste.

Garlic Yogurt Sauce

1 cup plain yogurt
1 clove garlic, minced
¼ teaspoon salt
½ teaspoon crushed dried mint, or
    1 teaspoon minced fresh mint (optional)

Place the yogurt in a bowl. Mash the garlic with the salt to form a paste and add it to the yogurt. Mix well. If you are using the dried mint, mash it in with the garlic and salt. If you have fresh mint, add it to the sauce. Serve with fried eggplant or zucchini or with lamb dishes.

Yield: 1 cup.

Sauce For Meat

1 cup thick yogurt**
2 tablespoons Dijon-type mustard
2 teaspoons Worcestershire
1 teaspoon soy sauce

Mix all ingredients and serve with hot or cold meat or chicken.

**See page 16.

Sauce For Fish

½ cup thick yogurt**
¼ cup mayonnaise
3 egg whites
Grated rind of 1 lemon
Pinch of paprika
Few drops of lemon juice

Combine the thick yogurt with the mayonnaise. Beat the egg whites until they are fairly stiff. Fold them into the thick yogurt and mayonnaise. Season with the lemon rind, paprika and a few drops of lemon juice.

Yield: About 1½ cups.

**See page 16.

Watercress Sauce

1 cup drained yogurt**
1 cup minced watercress leaves
½ cup minced parsley
1 tablespoon minced onion
1 tablespoon lemon juice
Salt and pepper to taste

Blend all ingredients thoroughly. Chill briefly before serving. Good with meat, poultry or fish.

Yield: 2 cups.

**See page 16.

Horseradish Sauce

Combine 1 cup thick yogurt** with ½ cup grated fresh horse-radish or with thoroughly drained bottled horseradish to taste. Serve with hot or cold meats, or on a baked potato. Add some to applesauce as a side dish with meat.

Yield: 1½ cups.

**See page 16.

Breads, Loaf Cakes and Cookies

White Bread

1 envelope dry yeast (2½ teaspoons)
½ cup warm water (105-115°)
1 teaspoon sugar
2 tablespoons butter
½ cup lukewarm yogurt
3 cups unbleached flour, or
    2 cups unbleached flour and
    1 cup cake flour
1 teaspoon salt

Dissolve the yeast in the warm water with the sugar, and let stand for about 10 minutes, until the liquid is foamy.

Melt the butter and add it to the yogurt, blending well.

In a large bowl, mix the yeast and water with the yogurt and butter. Beat in the flour and salt.

Turn out on a floured surface and knead thoroughly, about 8 to 10 minutes. This is a somewhat soft dough.

Wash the bowl, grease it and return the kneaded dough to it. Cover with a damp towel or a piece of buttered plastic or foil, and set in a warm draft-free spot to rise for about 1½ to 2 hours.

When doubled in bulk, punch down, form into a loaf and place in a buttered 9" x 5" x 3" loaf pan. Slash the top with a razor or sharp knife, cover with a towel and let rise until doubled, about 1½ to 2 hours.

Preheat the oven to 350°.

Bake until the loaf sounds hollow when rapped, about 35 minutes.

Yield: 1 loaf.

Wheat Germ Bread

½ cup warm yogurt (105-115°)
½ cup warm water (105-115°)
1 envelope dry yeast (2½ teaspoons)
1 teaspoon sugar
1 cup unbleached flour
1 cup whole wheat flour
¾ cup cake flour (see Note)
¼ cup wheat germ
1 teaspoon salt

In a deep bowl, mix the yogurt and water. Stir in the yeast and sugar and let stand for about 10 minutes, until the liquid is foamy.

Combine the flours with the wheat germ and salt. Beat half the flour mixture into the yeast mixture, then add the balance of the flour mixture.

Turn the dough out on a lightly floured surface and knead thoroughly for about 8 to 10 minutes, until the dough feels smooth and elastic. This is a somewhat stiff dough. Form into a ball.

Wash the bowl, oil it lightly and put the ball of dough in the bowl, turning it so that the entire surface is lightly oiled. Cover the bowl with a damp towel or a piece of buttered plastic or foil and set it in a warm draft-free spot to double in bulk, about 2 to 2½ hours.

When the dough has risen, punch down and remove to a floured surface. Form into a loaf and place in a lightly greased 9" x 5"x 3" loaf pan. Slash the top with a razor or sharp knife. Cover with a towel and let rise until doubled, about 2 to 2½ hours.

Preheat the oven to 400°.

Spray or paint the top with water just before placing in the lower third of the oven. Bake until the loaf sounds hollow when rapped, about 30 to 35 minutes.

Yield: 1 loaf.

Note: Cake flour can be omitted and the unbleached flour increased by ¾ cup.

Banana-Nut Bread

½ cup butter
1 cup sugar
2 eggs
1¼ cups mashed very ripe bananas
*   (2 large or 3 small)*
1/3 cup yogurt
2 cups sifted all-purpose flour
*   (sift before measuring)*
1 teaspoon baking soda
¼ teaspoon salt
½ cup chopped walnuts

Preheat the oven to 350°.

Cream the butter with the sugar until light and fluffy. Add the eggs, beating after each addition.

Combine the mashed bananas with the yogurt, mixing well.

Sift the flour with the baking soda and salt.

Add the flour mixture and the banana-and-yogurt mixture alternately to the butter-and-sugar mixture. Stir in the chopped nuts.

Turn into a greased and lightly floured 8½" x 4½" x 2-5/8" loaf pan. Bake until a cake tester inserted in the center comes out clean, about 1 hour.

Let cool in pan for about 10 minutes before turning out onto a rack. When completely cool, wrap it in plastic or foil and store it at room temperature for 24 hours before slicing.

Yield: 1 loaf.

Whole Wheat Banana Bread

½ cup butter
¾ cup brown sugar
1 egg
1 cup sifted whole wheat flour
   (sift before measuring)
½ cup sifted all-purpose flour
   (sift before measuring)
1 teaspoon baking soda
¼ teaspoon salt
1¼ cups mashed very ripe bananas
   (2 large or 3 small)
¼ cup yogurt
½ cup raisins

Preheat the oven to 350°.

Cream the butter with the sugar until light and fluffy. Beat in the egg.

Sift the flours with the baking soda and salt.

Combine the mashed bananas with the yogurt, mixing thoroughly. Add the flour mixture and the banana-and-yogurt mixture alternately to the butter-and-sugar mixture. Stir in the raisins.

Turn into a greased and floured 8½" x 2½" x 2-5/8" loaf pan. Bake until a cake tester inserted in the center comes out clean, about 1 hour. Cool in the pan for about 10 minutes before turning out on a rack.

Yield: 1 loaf.

Carrot Cake

6 tablespoons butter

1 2/3 cups sugar

3 eggs

2 cups sifted all-purpose flour
    (sift before measuring)

2 teaspoons baking soda

½ teaspoon salt

½ teaspoon cinnamon

1 cup yogurt

2 cups grated carrots (5 or 6 medium carrots)

1 cup chopped walnuts

1 cup shredded coconut (optional)

Preheat the oven to 350°.

Cream the butter with the sugar. Add the eggs, beating after each addition, until well blended.

Sift the flour with the baking soda, salt and cinnamon.

Add the flour mixture and the yogurt alternately to the butter-and-egg mixture.

Fold in the carrots, nuts and coconut, stirring lightly until they are just mixed throughout the batter.

Pour the batter into a greased and lightly floured 13" x 9" x 2" or 9" x 5" x 3" pan or into 4 baby loaf pans (5¾" x 3¼" x 2"). Bake until a cake tester inserted in the center comes out clean, about 55 minutes for the rectangle or baby loaves, about an hour and 10 minutes for the large loaf.

Cool the cake in the pan for about 10 minutes before turning it out on a rack. When cook, wrap in plastic or foil and store at room temperature for 24 hours before slicing or cutting.

Yield: 1 large cake or loaf, or 4 small loaves.

Corn Bread

¾ cup yellow cornmeal
1 cup all-purpose flour
1 tablespoon sugar
1 teaspoon baking powder
1 teaspoon baking soda
½ teaspoon salt
1 egg, beaten
1 cup yogurt
2 tablespoons bacon drippings
* or melted butter*

Preheat the oven to 450°.

Sift together the cornmeal, flour, sugar, baking powder, baking soda and salt.

Combine the beaten egg and yogurt, and add them to the dry ingredients. Add the bacon drippings or melted butter and stir the batter lightly.

Turn into a greased 9-inch square baking pan and bake in the middle of the oven for about 30 minutes until tester comes out clean. Serve hot.

Yield: One 9-inch square.

Cranberry-Orange Bread

Rind and juice of 1 orange
(1 teaspoon rind, 1/3 cup juice)
2 tablespoons melted butter
1/3 cup yogurt
1 cup coarsely chopped cranberries
½ cup chopped walnuts
2 cups sifted all-purpose flour
(sift before measuring)
1 cup sugar
1½ teaspoons baking powder
½ teaspoon baking soda
½ teaspoon salt

Preheat the oven to 350°.

In a measuring cup, combine the orange rind and juice with the melted butter and yogurt. Set aside.

Combine the cranberries and nuts, and set them aside.

Sift the flour with the sugar, baking powder, baking soda and salt.

Add the juice-and-yogurt mixture to the flour-and-sugar mixture, combining them thoroughly. Mix in the chopped cranberries and nuts and turn into a greased and lightly floured 8½" x 2½" x 2-5/8" loaf pan. Bake until a cake tester inserted in the center comes out clean, about 1 hour.

Let the bread cool in the pan for 10 minutes before turning it out onto a rack. When completely cool, wrap in plastic or foil and store at room temperature for 24 hours before slicing.

Yield: 1 loaf.

Date-Nut Loaf

¾ cup butter
¾ cup light brown sugar
2 eggs
2¾ cups sifted all-purpose flour
   (sift before measuring)
2 teaspoons baking powder
1 teaspoon baking soda
¾ teaspoon cinnamon
½ teaspoon salt
1 cup yogurt
8 ounces chopped pitted dates
¾ cups chopped walnuts

Preheat the oven to 350°.

Cream the butter with the sugar until light and fluffy, and beat in the eggs.

Sift the flour with the baking powder, baking soda, cinnamon and salt.

Add the flour mixture and the yogurt alternately to the butter-and-sugar mixture, beginning and ending with the flour. Stir in the dates and nuts.

Turn into a greased and lightly floured 9" x 5" x 3" loaf pan or other 8-cup pan. Bake until a cake tester inserted in the center comes out clean, about 1 hour.

Cool in the pan for about 10 minutes before turning out on a rack. When completely cook, wrap in plastic or foil and store at room temperature for 24 hours before slicing.

Yield: 1 loaf.

Honey Wheat Bread

1 cup honey
1 cup yogurt
4 tablespoons butter
2 eggs, lightly beaten
1¼ cups sifted all-purpose flour
    (sift before measuring)
1¼ cups sifted whole wheat flour
    (sift before measuring)
2 teaspoons baking powder
1 teaspoon baking soda
½ teaspoon salt
½ cup chopped walnuts or pecans
½ cup raisins (optional)

Preheat the oven to 325°.

In a saucepan, combine the honey and yogurt and heat over moderate heat, stirring until they are thoroughly blended. Cut up the butter and add the pieces to the pan. Stir until the butter is melted. Remove the pan from the heat and let the mixture cool slightly before adding the beaten eggs (if the mixture is too hot, the eggs will start to cook).

Sift the flours with the baking powder, baking soda and salt. Stir the flour mixture into the liquid, beating lightly until smooth and well blended. Fold in the nuts and raisins.

Pour the batter into a greased and floured 8½" x 4½" x 2-5/8" loaf pan or into 3 baby loaf pans (5¾" x 3¼" x 2") Bake in the middle of the oven until a cake tester comes out clean, about 1¼ hours for the large loaf or about 45 minutes for the smaller loaves. Allow the cake to cool in the pan for about 15 minutes before turning it out on a rack.

Yield: 1 large or 3 small loaves.

Lemon Tea Loaf

6 tablespoons butter
1 cup sugar
2 eggs
Grated rind of 1 lemon
1 teaspoon lemon extract
Pinch of salt
1½ cups sifted all-purpose flour
   (sift before measuring)
½ teaspoon baking soda
½ teaspoon baking powder
½ cup plain yogurt
1/3 cup sugar
Juice of 1 lemon

Preheat the oven to 350°.

Cream together the butter and 1 cup sugar. Add the eggs and beat until light and fluffy. Add the lemon rind, lemon extract and salt, and mix well.

Sift the flour with the baking soda and baking powder.

Stir the flour mixture and the yogurt alternately into the butter-and-sugar mixture, beginning and ending with the flour.

Pour the batter into a greased and very lightly floured 8½" x 4½" x 2-5/8" loaf pan. Bake until a cake tester inserted in the center comes out clean, about 1¼ hours.

While the cake is baking, dissolve the 1/3 cup sugar in the lemon juice in a small pan. Place the pan over low heat and stir gently until the sugar is completely dissolved.

When the cake is done, place the loaf pan on a rack. Pour the lemon-and-sugar syrup over the hot cake while it is in the pan. Allow the cake to cool completely in the pan before removing it.

Yield: 1 loaf.

Prune-Nut Bread

8 ounces dried prunes
4 tablespoons butter
½ cup sugar
1 egg
1½ cups sifted all-purpose flour
   (sift before measuring)
1 teaspoon baking soda
½ teaspoon salt
1½ cups sifted whole wheat flour
   (sift before measuring)
1 cup yogurt
1 cup broken nuts

Simmer the prunes for about 20 minutes in enough water to cover them or until they are soft. Add more water during cooking, if necessary, to keep them covered. Mash the cooked prunes or put them through a blender or food mill to make a pulp. You will need ¾ cup pulp. Measure ¼ cup of the prune cooking liquid and set aside.

Preheat the oven to 350°.

Cream the butter with the sugar and beat in the egg. Add the prune pulp and juice and mix well.

Sift the all-purpose flour with the baking soda and salt, and add to this the sifted whole wheat flour.

Add the flour mixture and the yogurt alternately to the butter-and-prune mixture. Stir only enough to blend. Fold in the broken nuts.

Turn into a greased 8½" x 4½" x 2-5/8" loaf pan. Bake until a cake tester inserted in the center comes out clean.

Cool in the pan for 10 minutes before turning out on a rack. When cool, wrap in plastic or foil and store at room temperature for 24 hours before slicing.

Yield: 1 loaf.

Irish Soda Bread

3 cups all-purpose flour
½ cup sugar
2 teaspoons baking powder
1 teaspoon baking soda
1 teaspoon salt
¼ pound butter (1 stick)
2 eggs, beaten
1 cup yogurt mixed with ¼ cup water
2 tablespoons caraway seeds
1 cup raisins
½ cup currants
1 tablespoon melted butter
1 tablespoon sugar
1 tablespoon milk

Preheat the oven to 375°.

Sift the flour, ½ cup sugar, baking powder, baking soda and salt into a large bowl. Work the ¼ pound butter into the flour until the mixture is crumblike.

Add the eggs and the yogurt mixed with water. Stir in the caraway seeds, raisins and currants.

Grease a heavy skillet (9-inch cast-iron is ideal), and turn the batter into the skillet. With a sharp knife dipped in flour, make 2 cuts in the form of a cross on the top. Bake in the middle of the oven for about 40 minutes until it sounds hollow when tapped. While the bread is baking, make a glaze with the melted butter, 1 tablespoon sugar and the milk. When the bread is done, remove it from the oven. Turn the bread out of the skillet to cool on a rack and brush it with the glaze.

Yield: One 9-inch-round loaf.

Whole Wheat Soda Bread

1½ cups whole wheat flour
½ cup all-purpose flour
1 teaspoon salt
½ teaspoon baking powder
½ teaspoon baking soda
¾ cup yogurt mixed with ¼ cup water

Preheat the oven to 375°.

Sift the flours with the salt, baking powder and baking soda. Add the yogurt-and-water mixture, and work it into the flour mixture.

Turn the dough onto a floured board and quickly work it into a round about 1 inch thick. Try not to handle the dough too much. With a sharp knife dipped in flour or with a razor blade, make 2 deep cuts in the top of the loaf in the form of a cross.

Place the dough on a greased griddle or cookie sheet. Bake in the middle of the oven until it sounds hollow when rapped, about 40 minutes. Cool on a rack.

Yield: 1 loaf about 8 inches in diameter.

Myrtie's Spice Cake

¼ pound butter (1 stick)
1½ cups brown sugar
2 eggs, beaten
1¾ cups sifted all-purpose flour
*   (sift before measuring)*
1 teaspoon baking soda
¼ teaspoon salt
1 teaspoon cinnamon
½ teaspoon nutmeg
½ teaspoon ground cloves
1 cup yogurt
½ cup chopped nuts
½ cup raisins

Preheat the oven to 350°.

Cream the butter with the sugar and add the eggs, beating well.

Sift the flour with the baking soda, salt and spices.

Add the flour mixture and the yogurt alternately to the butter-and-sugar mixture. Fold in the nuts and raisins.

Pour into a greased floured 8½" x 4½" x 2-5/8" loaf pan or an 8" x 8" x 2" square pan. Bake until a cake tester inserted in the center comes out clean, about 45 minutes. Let cool in the pan for 10 minutes before turning out on a rack.

Yield: 1 loaf or one 8-inch-square cake.

Chocolate Chip Cookies

6 tablespoons butter
1/3 cup brown sugar, or 3 tablespoons
brown sugar and 3 tablespoons
white sugar
1 egg
½ teaspoon vanilla extract
1¼ cups sifted all-purpose flour
(sift before measuring)
½ teaspoon baking soda
¼ teaspoon salt
¼ cup yogurt
One 6-ounce package chocolate bits

Preheat the oven to 375°.

Cream the butter and add the sugar, beating until the mixture is light and fluffy. Add the egg and vanilla and beat until blended.

Sift the flour with the baking soda and salt and add it alternately with the yogurt to the butter-and-sugar mixture, beginning and ending with the flour. Stir in the chocolate bits.

Drop by rounded teaspoonfuls onto greased cookie sheets and bake in the middle of the oven for about 10 to 12 minutes until lightly browned. Remove the cookies from the cookie sheet and let them cool on a rack.

Yield: About 3 dozen.

Chocolate Nut Cookies

2 squares (2 ounces) semisweet chocolate
11 tablespoons butter·
1 1/3 cups sugar
1 egg
1 teaspoon vanilla extract
½ cup thick yogurt**
2 cups sifted all-purpose flour
    (sift before measuring)
½ teaspoon baking soda
½ teaspoon baking powder
¼ teaspoon salt
½ cup chopped walnuts, pecans or peanuts

Preheat the oven to 375°.

Melt the chocolate in a bowl set over hot water or in the top of a double boiler over hot water. Let it cool.

Cream the butter and add the sugar, blending it until creamy. Add the egg and vanilla and mix until fluffy. Stir in the chocolate and thick yogurt, mixing well.

Sift the flour with the baking soda, baking powder and salt, and add it, mixing well. Stir in the nuts.

Drop by teaspoonfuls onto greased cookie sheets. Bake in the middle of the oven for about 12 to 15 minutes or until top is crisp.

Remove the cookies from the cookie sheets and let them cool on a rack.

Yield: 4 dozen.

**See page 16.

Drop Cookies

4 tablespoons butter
1 cup sugar
1 egg, lightly beaten
1 teaspoon grated lemon or orange rind
¼ cup yogurt
1¼ cups sifted all-purpose flour
  (sift before measuring)
½ teaspoon salt
¼ teaspoon baking soda
¼ teaspoon baking powder

Preheat the oven to 375°.

Cream the butter and sugar and beat in the egg, grated rind and yogurt.

Sift the flour with the salt, baking soda and baking powder. Add the flour mixture to the butter-and-sugar mixture.

Drop by teaspoonfuls onto greased cookie sheets (not too close together). Bake for about 15 minutes or until lightly colored. Remove the cookies from the cookie sheets and cool on a rack.

Yield: about 40.

Date Drop Cookies

¼ pound butter (1 stick)
½ cup sifted brown sugar
    (sift before measuring)
1 cup light molasses
2/3 cup thick yogurt**
1 teaspoon grated lemon rind
3 cups sifted all-purpose flour
    (sift before measuring)
2 teaspoons baking soda
½ teaspoon salt
1 cup chopped dates

Preheat the oven to 375°.

Cream the butter and sugar, and beat until the mixture is fluffy. Beat in the molasses, thick yogurt and grated lemon rind.

Sift together the flour, baking soda and salt. Toss a quarter of this mixture with the chopped dates. Add the floured dates and the rest of the flour mixture to the butter-and-sugar mixture. Combine thoroughly.

Drop by tablespoonfuls onto 2 greased cookie sheets and bake in the middle level of the oven for about 15 minutes or until well-browned and springy to the touch. Remove the cookies from the cookie sheets and cool on a rack.

Yield: 3½ dozen.

**See page 16.

Hermits

¼ pound butter (1 stick)
1 cup brown sugar (sift before measuring)
1 egg, lightly beaten
½ cup yogurt

1 1/3 cups sifted all-purpose flour
   (sift before measuring)
¼ teaspoon baking soda
¾ teaspoon cinnamon
½ teaspoon ground cloves
¼ cup broken walnuts or pecans
½ cup raisins (chopped if you like)

Preheat the oven to 375°.

Cream the butter and sugar until the mixture is soft and creamy. Beat in the egg and yogurt.

Sift the flour with the baking soda and spices. Add to the butter-and-sugar mixture and beat until smooth. Stir in the nuts and raisins.

Drop by teaspoonfuls onto greased cookie sheets and bake for about 15 minutes until brown and almost firm. Remove the cookies from the cookie sheets and cool on a rack.

Yield: About 2½ dozen.

Oatmeal Cookies

¾ cup butter (1½ sticks)
1 cup brown sugar
½ cup granulated sugar
1 egg, lightly beaten
¼ cup yogurt
1 teaspoon vanilla extract
1 cup sifted all-purpose flour
   (sift before measuring)
1 teaspoon salt
½ teaspoon baking soda
3 cups rolled oats

Preheat the oven to 350°.

Cream the butter with the sugars and add the beaten egg, beating until the mixture is creamy. Add the yogurt and vanilla.

Sift the flour with the salt and baking soda. Add the flour mixture to the butter-and-sugar mixture, blending thoroughly. Stir in the oats, blending well.

Drop by teaspoonfuls onto greased cookie sheets. Flatten the cookies slightly with the back of a fork or spoon dipped in cold water. Bake for about 12 to 15 minutes or until lightly browned. Remove the cookies from the cookie sheets and cool on a rack.

Yield: 4 dozen.

Spiced Oatmeal Cookies

¼ pound butter (1 stick)
½ cup brown sugar, firmly packed
1 egg, beaten
2 tablespoons yogurt
1 cup sifted all-purpose flour
   (sift before measuring)
½ teaspoon salt
¼ teaspoon baking soda
¼ teaspoon nutmeg
1/8 teaspoon ground cloves
¾ cup rolled oats
½ cup chopped nuts or raisins,
   or a combination of both

Preheat the oven to 375°.

Cream the butter with the sugar, and add the beaten egg and yogurt.

Sift the flour with the salt, baking soda and spices. Add the flour mixture to the butter-and-sugar mixture, blending thoroughly. Stir in the oats, mixing well. Stir in the nuts or raisins.

Drop by teaspoonfuls onto greased and floured cookie sheets. Flatten the cookies slightly with the back of a fork dipped in cold water. Chill the cookies for 30 minutes.

Bake until nicely browned, about 15 to 20 minutes. Remove the cookies from the cookie sheets and cool on a rack.

Yield: 3 dozen.

Peanut Butter Cookies

½ cup brown sugar
½ cup granulated sugar
¼ pound butter (1 stick)
1 egg
¾ cup smooth peanut butter
¼ cup yogurt cheese**
1½ cups sifted all-purpose flour
   (sift before measuring)
½ teaspoon salt
½ teaspoon baking soda
½ teaspoon vanilla extract

Preheat the oven to 375°.

Sift the sugars together. Cream the butter and add the sugars, mixing until creamy. Beat in the egg. Add the peanut butter and yogurt cheese, blending thoroughly.

Sift the flour with the salt and baking soda. Stir the flour mixture into the peanut butter mixture and add the vanilla.

Scoop up teaspoonfuls of dough and, with your hands, form small balls. Place them on ungreased cookie sheets. Press them flat with the back of a fork dipped in cold water and bake for about 15 minutes or until lightly colored. Remove the cookies from the cookie sheets and cool on a rack.

Yield: 4 dozen.

**See page 16.

Refrigerator Cookies

¼ pound butter (1 stick)
1 cup sugar
1 egg, beaten
1/3 cup yogurt cheese**
2 tablespoons yogurt
1 teaspoon vanilla extract
2 cups sifted all-purpose flour
    (sift before measuring)
½ teaspoon baking powder
½ teaspoon salt
¼ teaspoon baking soda
Sugar or a combination of sugar and cinnamon

Cream the butter and add the sugar and the beaten egg. Soften the yogurt cheese by mashing it with a fork and add the yogurt to it. Combine this mixture with the butter-and-sugar mixture and beat in the vanilla.

Sift the flour with the baking powder, salt and baking soda. Beat the flour mixture into the yogurt mixture. If the dough is too soft to form into a roll, chill it until it is firm enough. Form it into a roll 2 inches thick, wrap it in wax paper and refrigerate for at least 6 hours.

Preheat the oven to 350°.

Slice the roll into 1/8-inch rounds and sprinkle them with sugar or sugar mixed with cinnamon. Place the rounds on greased cookie sheets. Bake for about 12 minutes or until lightly browned. Remove the cookies from the cookie sheets and cool on a rack.

Yield: About 5 dozen.

Note: This dough can be frozen.

**See page 16.

Spiced Refrigerator Cookies

¼ pound butter (1 stick)
½ cup brown sugar
1¼ cups sifted all-purpose flour
  (sift before measuring)
1/8 teaspoon salt
1/8 teaspoon baking soda
1 teaspoon cinnamon
¼ teaspoon ground cloves
¼ teaspoon nutmeg
2 tablespoons thick yogurt**
½ cup chopped nuts

Cream the butter and sugar.

Sift the flour with the salt, baking soda and spices. Add the flour mixture and thick yogurt alternately to the butter-and-sugar mixture. Beat in the nuts and form the dough into a roll with floured hands. If it is too soft to form into a roll, chill it until it is firm enough. Form into a roll 2 inches thick, wrap it in wax paper and refrigerate it for at least 12 hours.

Preheat the oven to 375°.

Slice the roll into 1/8-inch rounds. Bake them on greased cookie sheets for about 12 minutes or until lightly browned. Remove the cookies from the cookie sheets and cool on a rack.

Yield: About 40.

**See page 16.

Desserts

Cold Apricot Soufflé

One 8-ounce package dried apricots
1 envelope unflavored gelatin
½ cup water or apricot juice
½ cup thick yogurt**
6 eggs
1/3 cup sugar
1 tablespoon Grand Marnier,
    or 1 teaspoon orange extract
¼ teaspoon cream of tartar
2 tablespoons sugar
½ cup yogurt cream**

Cover the apricots with boiling water and soak them for about 30 minutes in a saucepan. Add as much additional water as necessary to just cover them and cook them over very low heat for about 25 to 30 minutes, until they are very soft and easily mashed.

Soften the gelatin in the ½ cup water or apricot juice.

In a blender, puree the apricots with the thick yogurt and scrape the mixture into a large mixing bowl.

Separate the eggs, dropping the whites into a large clean bowl, and the yolks into the top part of a double boiler. Beat the yolks lightly, gradually adding the 1/3 cup sugar. Place the pan over boiling water and stir the yolk-and-sugar mixture continuously until it thickens. Do not let the yolks cook. If the mixture starts to get lumpy, immediately remove the pan from over the boiling water and stir vigorously for a minute or two before returning to the boiling water.

When the yolk mixture is thick and will coat a spoon with a creamy layer, remove the pan from heat and stir for a few minutes to cool. Add the Grand Marnier or orange extract.

Place the softened gelatin in a saucepan over low heat and stir until the gelatin is thoroughly dissolved. Beat it into the yolk mixture. When well blended, add this mixture to the apricot-and-yogurt mixture, stirring well.

Beat the egg whites with a pinch of salt and the cream of tartar, adding the 2 tablespoons of sugar gradually at the end. The whites should form peaks and be stiff but not dry. Fold the egg whites into the apricot mixture.

Whip the yogurt cream and fold it into the apricot mixture.

Pour into a 6-cup mold (which has been rinsed in cold water), a glass bowl or individual bowls. Let chill for at least 4 hours or overnight.

Yield: 8 to 10 servings.

**See page 16.

Cold Orange Soufflé Denis

2 eggs, separated
½ cup sugar (preferably superfine)
One 6-ounce can frozen orange juice
*   concentrate*
1 tablespoon water
1 envelope unflavored gelatin
¼ cup water
1 tablespoon Grand Marnier
*2 cups drained yogurt***
1/8 teaspoon cream of tartar

Beat the egg yolks and ¼ cup of the sugar in the top part of a double boiler set over boiling water until the mixture is thick, lemon colored and ribbony. Add the orange juice concentrate. Rinse out the can with 1 tablespoon water and add this water to the mixture. Stir and let the mixture thicken until it coats a spoon. Remove the pan from the heat to let cool slightly.

Place the gelatin and ¼ cup water in a saucepan over low heat, and stir until the gelatin is dissolved. Add the dissolved gelatin and the Grand Marnier to the cooled yolk-and-orange mixture. Chill over ice or in the refrigerator until it begins to set.

Beat the egg whites with a pinch of salt and the cream of tartar, adding the remaining ¼ cup of sugar gradually at the end. The whites should form peaks and be stiff but not dry. Stir a quarter of the egg whites into the orange mixture to lighten it. Then fold in the rest of the whites.

Pour the mixture into a small serving dish. Chill in the refrigerator for about 2 or 3 hours before serving.

Yield: 4 servings.

**See page 16.

Baked Lemon Pudding

3 eggs, separated
1½ cups sugar
¼ cup fresh lemon juice
2 teaspoons grated lemon rind
1/3 cup flour
Pinch of salt
1½ cups yogurt
¼ teaspoon cream of tartar
1 teaspoon butter

Preheat the oven to 300°.

In the top of a double boiler, blend the egg yolks, sugar, lemon juice and rind, flour, salt and yogurt. Cook over simmering water, stirring continuously, until the mixture is thick and smooth. Remove from heat and allow to cool slightly.

Beat the egg whites with the cream of tartar and a pinch of salt until they form peaks and are stiff but not dry. Fold the whites into the lemon mixture.

Pour into a lightly buttered 6-cup baking dish. Set the baking dish in a pan of hot water in the lower third of the oven and bake until set, about 1 hour.

Coeur à la Crème

2 cups yogurt cheese**
1 cup yogurt cream**
Fresh strawberries or raspberries
Powdered sugar

Mash the yogurt cheese and mix it well with the yogurt cream until smooth.

Line a heart-shaped perforated 3-cup mold or a basket with cheesecloth. (A small round or oval basket can be substituted, although it will no longer be a "coeur.")

Press the cheese mixture into the lined mold and place it over a bowl in the refrigerator; let it drain for several hours.

Unmold onto a chilled plate and surround with strawberries or raspberries dusted with powdered sugar.

Yield: 6 servings.

**See page 16.

Grapes and Blueberries

1 pint blueberries
1 small bunch seedless grapes
Thick yogurt** or whipped yogurt cream**
Brown sugar

Wash the blueberries and grapes, mix them together and chill for several hours. Top each serving of fruit with a large dollop of thick yogurt or whipped yogurt cream and sprinkle generously with brown sugar.

Yield: 4 servings.

**See page 16.

Chocolate Cake

¼ pound butter (1 stick)
1 cup sugar
1 egg
½ teaspoon vanilla extract
1½ cups sifted cake flour
   (sift before measuring)
1/3 cup cocoa
1 teaspoon baking soda
½ teaspoon salt
1 cup yogurt

Butter an 8" x 8" x 2" cake pan and line the bottom with waxed paper. Butter the paper.

Preheat the oven to 350°.

Cream the butter and add the sugar, beating until light and fluffy. Add the egg and beat well. Stir in the vanilla.

Sift together the cake flour, cocoa, baking soda and salt. Add to the butter-and-sugar mixture alternately with the yogurt, beginning and ending with the dry ingredients.

Pour the batter into the prepared cake pan and bake in the middle of the oven until a cake tester inserted in the center comes out clean, about 25 to 30 minutes. Allow the cake to cool in the pan for about 5 minutes before turning it out on a rack.

After it has cooled, dust the cake with powdered sugar, spread it with a thin layer of apricot jam and dust it with powdered sugar, or spread it with a thin layer of orange marmalade topped with a thin layer of chocolate frosting.

Yield: One 8-inch-square cake.

Peanut Butter Cake

6 tablespoons butter
1½ cups brown sugar
2 eggs, lightly beaten
½ cup peanut butter (preferably chunky)
1 teaspoon vanilla extract
2 cups sifted all-purpose flour
   (sift before measuring)
1½ teaspoons baking powder
½ teaspoon baking soda
½ teaspoon salt
¾ cup yogurt

Preheat the oven to 350°.

Cream the butter with the sugar until smooth and fluffy. Beat in the eggs and peanut butter, and mix well. Add the vanilla.

Sift the flour with the baking powder, baking soda and salt.

Add the flour mixture and the yogurt alternately to the butter-and-sugar mixture, mixing well. Pour the batter into a greased 8" x 8" x 2" pan. Bake in the middle of the oven until a cake tester inserted in the center comes out clean, about 40 minutes. Let the cake cool in the pan for 15 minutes before turning it out on a rack.

Yield: One 8-inch-square cake.

Honey and Cheese Pie

1 cup yogurt cheese**
1 cup ricotta or cottage cheese
½ cup sugar
½ cup honey
3 eggs

1 teaspoon lemon juice
1 teaspoon grated lemon rind
1 prebaked 9-inch pie shell, cooled

Preheat the oven to 350°.

Mix the yogurt cheese with the ricotta or cottage cheese, the sugar and honey. Beat the eggs lightly and add them to the yogurt-and-cheese mixture with the lemon juice and rind. Mix very well.

Pour the mixture into the pie shell and bake until the filling is golden brown and shows cracks on the surface, about 45 minutes.

This is best served warm. If allowed to cool, it will sink slightly.

Yield: 8 servings.

**See page 16.

Ricotta Dessert

1 pound ricotta cheese
½ cup yogurt
2 to 3 tablespoons powdered sugar
3 tablespoons Grand Marnier, cognac, or rum
2 tablespoons fine grind coffee (Italian or French
roast) or instant coffee

Combine the ricotta with the yogurt and beat until the mixture is creamy. Gradually blend in the sugar. Add the liquor and blend until the mixture is the consistency of custard.

Place in individual serving bowls or 1 large serving bowl, and chill in the refrigerator for 2 hours or longer.

Just before serving, sprinkle the pulverized coffee over the top.

Yield: 6 servings.

Frozen Yogurt, Sweet Yogurt, and Beverages

Frozen Yogurt—What It Is

Much of the so-called frozen yogurt on the market today is not really yogurt. Very often it is a liquid dairy product containing many preservatives but no yogurt, run through a soft-ice-cream machine. Laws are being drawn up in some states to require that products called frozen yogurt must contain live yogurt culture. Freezing yogurt does not kill the yogurt culture but merely inhibits it. Pasteurizing the yogurt does kill the live culture.

Since yogurt in its natural state becomes icy when it is frozen, gelatin is added to help retain a creamy texture. An additional aid to achieving smoothness is to drain the yogurt, thereby reducing the liquid content and cutting down on the formation of ice crystals.

There is a frozen yogurt device on the market which is nonelectric and requires no rock salt. It is essentially a double-walled plastic tub with a refrigerant sealed into it. It has a cover and comes with a plastic dasher which is inserted at the end of the freezing time to soften the partially frozen yogurt. The plastic tub is placed in the freezer until the sealed refrigerant is solidly frozen (usually overnight). The yogurt mixture is placed in the tub and is ready to serve in 30 to 40 minutes. The dasher is inserted and turned backward and forward to soften the frozen mixture.

One could make a similar device with 2 plastic containers of slightly different sizes, placing one inside the other and freezing water in the space between their walls. The freezing time for the yogurt will vary according to the amount of yogurt, the efficiency of your freezer and the desired consistency.

The yogurt mixture can also be frozen in an ice tray. Whether you freeze it in your ice tray or in double-walled plastic containers, it will have to be beaten before serving in order to soften it. After 30 minutes or so of freezing, beat it with a wooden spoon to break up any icy formation. If it becomes too soft, return it to the freezing compartment to let it firm up. Beat again just before serving.

The yogurt can also be frozen in ice cube form, and the cubes can be stored in plastic bags in the freezer. An ice tray that freezes in slices rather than cubes would be preferable. The cubes should be allowed to thaw partially before you attempt to puree them in a blender. If the puree becomes softer than you like, return the mixture to the freezer to firm up. Stir vigorously before serving.

If you own a food processor, just toss the partially thawed cubes in the work bowl, puree them and serve. With a food processor, you can also puree fruit with sugar or honey to taste and freeze this puree in cube form. Store the cubes in a plastic bag in the freezer. When you want to have some frozen fruit yogurt, place the fruit cubes and yogurt in the work bowl and puree them together. I feel that this method produces the smoothest and creamiest frozen yogurt.

Frozen Vanilla Yogurt

1 quart skim milk plus ½ cup
   powdered skim milk, or
    1 quart whole milk
1/3 cup sugar
1 teaspoon vanilla extract
2 tablespoons yogurt
1 envelope unflavored gelatin
2 tablespoons water or whey
Fresh fruit

Heat the milk to the boil, remove from the heat and, if using powdered skim milk, add it along with the sugar and vanilla. Let the mixture cool to 110°, then add the yogurt and incubate as you do regular yogurt (see page 12). Refrigerate the yogurt mixture for 3 hours after it has incubated.

Following the directions on page 15, drain off 1 cup of whey from the yogurt mixture.

While the yogurt mixture is draining, soften the gelatin in the water or whey in a small bowl. Set the bowl in a pan of hot water over low heat and stir until the gelatin is completely dissolved.

Blend the dissolved gelatin into the drained yogurt (there should be 3 cups yogurt) by beating thoroughly or using a food processor or blender. Freeze according to the method you have selected. Serve topped with fresh fruit.

Yield: 3 cups (1½ pints).

Note: This is a delicious dessert in its unfrozen state. After blending the gelatin and the drained yogurt, turn it into a serving bowl and refrigerate it until it is set. Top with fresh fruit.

VARIATIONS

Follow the directions for Frozen Vanilla Yogurt substituting 1½ teaspoons orange or lemon extract for the vanilla extract.

Note: This too is delicious unfrozen.

Frozen Apricot Yogurt

6 ounces dried apricots
3 tablespoons sugar or honey
1 envelope unflavored gelatin
¼ cup water
3 cups yogurt

Place the apricots in a saucepan and pour boiling water over them to cover. Let the apricots soak, preferably overnight.

Add more water, if necessary, to cover apricots. Place the pan over moderate heat and bring to a boil. Lower the heat and let the apricots simmer for about 20 to 30 minutes, until they are very soft. Add the sugar or honey and stir to blend. Remove from heat and let the apricots cool slightly.

Soften the gelatin in ¼ cup water in a small bowl or the top part of a double boiler.

Puree the cooled apricots in a food processor or blender.

Place the bowl containing the softened gelatin in a small pan of hot water over low heat, stirring until the gelatin is completely dissolved. Or, if using the top part of a double boiler, place over boiling water to dissolve.

Add the gelatin to the apricot puree, blending well. Add the yogurt and blend in a food processor or blender. Freeze according to the method you have selected (see instructions on page 203).

Yield: 1 quart.

VARIATION

Substitute prunes for the apricots.

Frozen Banana Yogurt

Allow bananas to ripen until the skins have darkened. Chill the bananas in the refrigerator so they will peel more easily. Peel the bananas and wrap each one in plastic wrap. Freeze the bananas until they are hard.

For each serving, cut a frozen banana into thick slices and puree in a food processor or blender with ½ cup to 1 cup of yogurt (depending on the size of the banana and the consistency you want). Add a pinch of nutmeg. Garnish with sliced unfrozen banana or with strawberries.

Note: No sugar is needed for this frozen yogurt if you allow the bananas to ripen completely. When a banana is ripe, all its starch is converted to fruit sugar.

Frozen Strawberry Yogurt

1 pint strawberries (see Note)
3 tablespoons sugar or honey
1 envelope unflavored gelatin
¼ cup water
2½ cups drained yogurt**
Additional strawberries for garnish (optional)

Wash and hull the strawberries and puree them in a food processor or blender with the sugar or honey.

Soften the gelatin in the ¼ cup water in a small bowl or the top part of a double boiler. Place over hot water and stir until the gelatin is completely dissolved.

Add the dissolved gelatin to the strawberries and beat in the drained yogurt. Beat thoroughly until mixture is completely smooth (best done in a blender or food processor).

Freeze according to the method you have selected (see instructions on page 203).

Yield: 4 servings. If you want to serve 6, garnish each portion with fresh strawberries.

**See page 16.

Note: One 10-ounce package frozen sliced sweetened strawberries can be substituted for the fresh strawberries. Omit the sugar or honey. Thaw and puree the frozen strawberries, then proceed with the recipe.

VARIATION

Follow the recipe for Frozen Strawberry Yogurt (page 206), substituting ¾ pint blueberries for the pint of strawberries. Serve with the remaining blueberries as a garnish.

Yogurt Cream

1 cup (½ pint) heavy cream
1 teaspoon yogurt

Heat the cream to about 85°. Put the yogurt in a clean, warm glass jar. Add the warmed cream to the jar and mix it with the yogurt gently but thoroughly. Incubate as you do regular yogurt (see page 12). This cream can be whipped.

Yield: 1 cup (½ pint).

Vanilla Yogurt

2 cups (1 pint) whole milk (see Note)
2½ tablespoons sugar
½ teaspoon vanilla extract
1 tablespoon yogurt

Heat the milk to boiling; remove from heat and add the sugar and vanilla. Let the mixture cool to 110°. Mix with the yogurt and pour into a clean jar or jars. Incubate as you do regular yogurt (see page 12).

Yield: 2 cups (1 pint).

Note: You can substitute 2 cups skim milk and ¼ cup powdered non-fat milk for the 2 cups whole milk. Add the powdered milk after removing the milk from the heat and beat it in.

Honey Yogurt

2 cups (1 pint) whole milk
  (see Note above)
3 tablespoons honey
1 tablespoon yogurt

Heat the milk to boiling; remove from heat and add the honey, stirring to dissolve. Let the mixture cool to 110°. Mix with the . yogurt and pour into a clean jar or jars. Incubate as you do regular yogurt (see page 12).

Yield: 2 cups (1 pint).

Note: You can substitute 2 cups skim milk and ¼ cup powdered non-fat milk for the 2 cups whole milk. Add the powdered milk after removing the milk from the heat and beat it in.

Orange or Lemon Yogurt

2 cups (1 pint) whole milk
  (see Note opposite)
2½ tablespoons sugar
¾ teaspoon orange or lemon extract
1 tablespoon yogurt

Follow the directions for Vanilla Yogurt substituting orange or lemon extract for the vanilla extract.

Yield: 2 cups (1 pint).

Dried Fruit Yogurt

Cut up dried apricots or prunes, and stir them into 1 cup of yogurt. Let the fruit stay in the yogurt at least overnight to soak up the whey, making the yogurt thick and creamy and the fruit plump and juicy. Try this with other dried fruits such as apple or pear slices.

Fresh Fruit Yogurt

Stir halved or sliced strawberries, or cut-up fresh peaches into yogurt. Experiment with combinations of fruits, such as Bing cherries and bananas, bananas and oranges, or melon and blueberries.

Sweet Yogurt Sauce

Drain one of the sweet yogurts, such as honey, vanilla, orange or lemon (see page 208), until it has reached the consistency you want, and serve it as a sauce over fresh fruit or sliced loaf cake. See draining instructions on page 15.

Instant Breakfast Drink

Using a blender or a hand beater, combine:

½ cup orange juice
½ cup yogurt
1 raw egg

Yield: 1½ cups.

Tomato Shake

Using either a blender or a hand beater, combine:

1 cup chilled tomato, clam-and-tomato
*   or vegetable and tomato juice*
1 cup yogurt
Salt, pepper and lemon juice to taste
Curry powder to taste (optional)

Yield: 2 cups.

Orange-Honey Shake

Using either a blender or a hand beater, combine:

1 cup orange juice
1 cup yogurt
1 tablespoon honey (or to taste)

Yield: 2 cups.

Dook

A wonderfully refreshing drink on a hot day. Put 2 or 3 ice cubes in a tall glass and add 1 cup yogurt and a pinch of salt. Fill with club soda and stir.

Borani

Another refreshing, tangy drink similar to Dook (above), this is of Pakistani origin. Serve very cold, garnished with a strip of lemon peel. Using a blender or a hand beater, combine:

½ cup yogurt
1 cup club soda or water
Salt and pepper to taste
Pinch of chili powder or
*   few drops tabasco*
Pinch of dried mint or 1 small
*   mint leaf, chopped*

Yield: 1½ cups.

Banana Shake

In a blender or food processor, mash a frozen banana (see Frozen Banana Yogurt, page 206) with a cup or more of yogurt and a sprinkling of nutmeg.

Peach Shake

In a blender or food processor, puree a cut-up peeled peach with a cup or more of plain or vanilla yogurt. Add more sweetening, if you like.

VARIATIONS: Substitute strawberries or other fruits for the peach.

Substitute applesauce for the peach, and sprinkle with nutmeg or cinnamon.

Blueberry Shake

In a blender or food processor, combine:

1 cup yogurt
1 cup frozen unsweetened blueberries
½ teaspoon sugar (or to taste)
½ teaspoon vanilla extract

Yield: 2 cups.

LIQUID MEASURES

Cups, quarts, ounces, pounds, and
their metric equivalents

Nearest convenient equivalents (with nearest actual equivalents in parentheses)

Cups and Spoons	Quarts and Ounces	Metric Equivalents	French Terms
4 1/3 cups	1 quart 2 ounces (1.056 quarts)	1 liter 1,000 milliliters	1 litre
4 cups	1 quart	1 liter less 1 deciliter (0.946 liter)	. . .
2 cups (plus 2½ Tb)	17 ounces (16.907 ounces)	½ liter	demi-litre
2 cups	1 pint; 16 ounces	½ liter less 1½ Tb (0.473 liter)	. . .
1 cup (plus 1¼ Tb)	8 ounces (8.454 ounces)	¼ liter	quart de litre
1 cup	8 ounces	¼ liter (0.236 liter)	. . .
1/3 cup (plus 1 Tb)	3½ ounces (3.381 ounces)	1 deciliter 1/10 liter 100 mililiters	1 décilitre 1 demi-verre
1/3 cup	2 2/3 ounces	1 deciliter less 1 1/3 Tb (0.079 liter)	. . .
3 1/3 Tb	1¾ ounces (1.690 ounces)	½ deciliter 50 milliliters	demi-décilitre
1 Tb	½ ounce	15 milliliters 15 grams	cuillère a soupe or à bouche; verre à liqueur
2 tsp	1/3 ounce	10 milliliters 10 grams	cuillère à entremets
1 tsp	1/16 ounce	5 milliliters 5 grams	cuillère à café

Conversion Formulae: To convert: Quarts to liters, multiply the quarts by 0.94635; Liters into quarts, multiply the liters by 1.056688; Ounces into milliliters, multiply the ounces by 29.573; Milliliters into ounces, multiply the milliliters by 0.0338.

WEIGHTS
Pounds and ounces vs. metrics

POUNDS & OUNCES *(most convenient approximation)*	METRIC *(and usual French units underlined)*
2.2 pounds	1 kilogram—1,000 grams
1.1 pounds	500 grams (une livre)
1 pound (16 ounces)	464 grams
9 ounces	250 grams (une demi-livre)
½ pound (8 ounces)	227 grams
4 3/8 ounces	125 grams
¼ pound (4 ounces)	114 grams
3½ ounces	100 grams (un hecto—hectogramme)
2 2/3 ounces	75 grams
1¾ ounces	50 grams
1 ounce	30 grams (28.3 gr.)
1 scant ounce	25 grams
½ ounce	15 grams
1/3 ounce	10 grams
1/6 ounce	5 grams

Conversion Formulae: To convert: Ounces into grams, multiply the ounces by 28.3495; Grams into ounces, multiply the grams by 0.35274.

Index

Notes

Notes

Notes